FASCINATING

BIBLE
FACTS
PEOPLE, PLACES & EVENTS

David M. Howard, Jr., Ph.D.
Contributing Writer

Gary M. Burge, Ph.D.
Consultant

PUBLICATIONS INTERNATIONAL, LTD.

David M. Howard, Jr., is associate professor of Old Testament and Semitic Languages at Trinity Evangelical Divinity School and holds a Ph.D. in Near Eastern Studies from the University of Michigan. His writing credits include contributions to *The International Standard Bible Encyclopedia, Anchor Bible Dictionary,* and *Peoples of the Old Testament World.* He is a member of the Society of Biblical Literature and the Institute for Biblical Research.

Gary M. Burge is an associate professor in the Department of Biblical and Theological Studies at North Park College, Chicago. He holds a Ph.D. in New Testament from King's College, The University of Aberdeen, Aberdeen, Scotland, and a master of divinity from Fuller Theological Seminary, Pasadena. He is a member of the Biblical Archaeology Society.

ISBN: 0-7853-3261-8

Library of Congress Catalog Card Number: 92-60594

Picture credits:
Front cover: **The Crosiers** (top right); **Richard T. Nowitz** (top left, top right center, bottom left & bottom right); **Z. Radovan, Jerusalem** (top left center & bottom right center); **SuperStock** (center & bottom left center).

Back cover: **The Crosiers** (top); **Z. Radovan, Jerusalem** (bottom); **SuperStock:** Toledo Cathedral, Castile/Bridgeman Art Library, London (center).

Animals Animals: 73; Anthony Bannister: 134L; Mike Birkhead: 104T; Margot Conte: 134B; Zig Leszczynski: 130L; Robert Maier: 131B, 132B; Sean Morris: 140L; Noah Satat: 128R, 130T; Richard Shiell: 144C; Dr. Nigel Smith: 121R; Donald Specker: 145T; **AP/Wide World Photos:** 184B; **Art Resource:** 180B; Alinari: 36L, 37B, 47T, 93L, 93R, 227T, 258L, 259R, 264R; Borromeo: 167T; Foto Marburg: 17B, 28R, 46B, 91C, 178R, 238T, 240L, 257R; Giraudon: 21C, 35T, 45T, 54L, 95R, 115R, 138R, 187T, 213TR, 243T, 298T; Kavaler: 36R, 169T; Lauros-Giraudon: 245B; Scala: 17L, 20B, 40T, 41R, 44R, 45R, 47L, 50R, 57L, 66B, 70L, 74, 75T, 82R, 96T, 98T, 103T, 108L, 110T, 113L, 156T, 160L, 189B, 191B, 205T, 224R, 234B, 241R, 246B, 262R, 270T, 273T, 290B, 304T, 306R, 311B; SEF: 52B, 55L; Victoria & Albert Museum, London: 238R; **Bible Pictures:** 114T, 169R, 174T, 176T, 185B, 245T, 247T, 248B; **Biblical Archaeology Society:** 250R, 297B; Fred Anderegg: 175T; F.H.C. Birch: 315T; Daniel Blatt: 177T; Werner Braun: 61B, 68B, 149R, 204R C; Dan Cole: 49B, 178TL; Avinoam Danin: 145B, 210B; Courtesy of Paul Leslie Garber: 39L; Sonia Halliday: 49T, 97L, 188B, 282R, 303R; David Harris: 194, 214RC, 220T; Courtesy Israel Museum: 61T; Joint Sepphoris Project: 121T; Aharon Kempinski: 196L; Erich Lessing: 184T, 197R, 229B, 268T, 286T, 308R; Courtesy of Leon Levy Expedition/Carl Andrews: 179T; Ze'ev Meshel: 177C&B; Garo Nalbandian: 83L, 204LC; Richard T. Nowitz: 147, 151B; Patti O'Connor: 203T; Oriental Institute, University of Chicago: 296L; Avner Raban: 226L; Zev Radovan: 9B, 81B, 83B, 92T, 124L, 132L, 140B, 149L, 150T&L, 157R, 181B, 201L, 217C&B, 221T, 225BL, 228R, 229T, 254L; Hershel Shanks: 220BL; Jackie Silver: 178BL; Ephraim Stern: 180L; John C. Trever: 66L; Robert Wright: 85R; **Cambridge University**

Press: 57B; **The Crosiers:** 10C, 12B, 13T, 14T, 16L, 18L, 19T, 20C, 21B, 24R, 27B, 31R, 33L, 37T, 38B, 41L, 43R, 47R, 54R, 56T, 67B, 76C, 77LC, 80R, 81T, 83R, 89L, 97R, 103B, 106T, 116, 122L, 140R, 143T, 154B, 163T, 165C, 166L, 168R, 170R, 174B, 175C, 189R, 202L, 215L, 219L, 222T, 230, 241L, 243R, 244R, 250L, 252T, 254R, 256L, 260L, 262L, 264L&B, 266L, 282B, 297R, 310L; Connick Studios: 256R; Peter Dohman: 272L; **The Dore Bible Illustrations/Dover Publications, Inc. 1974:** 10B, 12T, 16R, 21T, 32R, 34T, 38R, 41T, 67L, 119R, 120B, 164, 172L, 188T, 213TL, 225BR, 236B, 253R, 302T; **FPG International:** 8T, 11R, 48B, 87T&B, 121L, 126L, 135T, 156B, 181T, 248L, 275B, 309T; J. Baker: 112B; Alex Bartel: 88L; Dave Bartruff: 60B; Gary Buss: 24L; David Butz: 129T; H. Carroll: 244B; P. Ciganovic: 45T; Robert Cundy: 99B; Arthur D'Amario III: 223TR; Paul Degreve: 285B; John Farrell: 51R; Wenzel Fischer: 128T; Charles M. Fitch: 127T; Lee Foster: 130R; Ray Garner: 180R; A. Giampiccolo: 59B, 192L; Maxine S. Goldenberg: 298B; John E. Gorman: 124R; Mark Greenberg: 113B; Farrell Grehan: 64C, 234T; Dennis Hallinan: 111B; Kiki Haynes: 123T; V. Henry: 268B; A. Himmelreich: 32B; Jim Howard: 276T; M.P. Kahl: 78T; Michael A. Keller: 34B; Michael Kornafel: 45L; Lee Kuhn: 132R, 139T; L.O.L., Inc.: 137B; L&M Photo: 22T; Kent Knudson: 115L; Guy Marche: 148T; James M. Mejuto: 123L; E. Nagele: 305B; M. Nelson: 25R; Richard T. Nowitz: 32L, 64B, 293L; O'Brien & Mayor Photography: 127B; Stan Osolinski: 79B; Eberhard E. Otto: 56B, 98B; Diane Payds: table of contents BR, 96B; R. Pleasant: 209T; Gary Randall: 117; H.G. Ross: 128B; Leonard Lee Rue: 137L; Adolf Schmidecker: 76B; Has Schneider: 209B; Monserrate Schwartz: 60R; Ulf Sjostedt: 278; 280T; Clyde H. Smith: 11L; D. Spindel: 13R, 28T, 65T; Jeffrey Sylvester: 58L; J. Taposchaner: 161T; The Telegraph Colour Library: 86B, 209C, 299L; Renuud Thomas: 15T; Travelpix: 155L; John Terence Turner: 59C, 133B; Jim Tuten: 79T, 119L; Michael L. Valeri: 168L; L. West: 126R; **The Image Bank:** 5; **NASA:** 165B; **International Stock Photography:** 120T, 186L; Ags Photography, Inc: 29T; Mark Bolster: 214T; Norris Clark: 99T; Peter Russell Clemens: 106B; J.G. Edmanson: 305R; Chad Ehlers: 104B; Johan Elbers: 91B; Tom & Michele Grimm: 123R, 126T; Judy Gurovitz: 205B; D. Kasterine: 60L; Kit Luce: 185L; Ronn Maratea Photography: 133T, 137R, 142T, 171R, 272T; Frank Maresca: 104C; John Michael: 100B, 208B; Donald L. Miller: 55B; Steve Myers: 142C; Tom O'Brien: 143R; Richard Pharaoh: 55R; Phyllis Picardi: 77RC; Will Regan Photography: 112T, 139B; Elliott Varner Smith: 283L; Wayne Sproul: 75C; Bill Stanton: 101T; Stockman: 281TL; Robert J. Stottlemyer: 134R; Peter Symasko: 182B; The Telegraphy Colour Library: 111R, 225T, 299R; Ryan Williams: 189L; Brent Winebrenner: 305L; Bobbe Wolf: 315L; **The New Testament/Dover Publications, Inc. 1986:** 25L, 53B, 70R, 111L, 207L, 225R; **Richard T. Nowitz:** table of contents LC, 4, 19L&R, 28L, 30L&R, 35C&B, 53T, 57R, 58T, 59T, 62B, 63L, 65R, 66R, 67R, 71T, 76T, 82L, 84B, 85B, 88R, 91T, 92B, 95L&B, 96C, 97C, 105, 114C, 118B, 125L, 128L, 131T, 135L, 139C, 142B, 144T&B, 146, 148C, 160B, 161B, 162L, 163B, 169L, 170L, 172R&B, 173R, 175B, 181R, 182R, 183T&B, 186R, 190B, 195, 196T, 203LC, 206C, 211T&LC, 212TL&B, 213B, 216B, 217T, 219R, 220BR, 221BR, 223TL, 223B, 224L, 227B, 228L, 235L, 236L, 237B, 239T, 250B, 255T, 257L, 260B, 265L, 271L, 273B, 277T&B, 280B, 283R&B, 284L&B, 285B, 287L&B, 288L, 289T&B, 290L, 291R&B, 292L, 293R, 294T&B, 295T, 297L, 300T&B, 302B, 304L, 306L&B, 307T&R, 308T, 309B, 311T, 312B, 313R&B, 314R; **PhotoEdit:** 65L, Bill Aron: 11B, 22B, 63R; Tony Freeman: 17R, 183C; John Neubauer: 15B; Alan Oddie: 64T, 82T, 291L; **Zev Radovan:** table of contents TL, TR, BL, 16B, 18R, 23L, 25T, 33R, 42B, 44L, 48T, 51B, 52L, 63T, 86L&R, 88B, 89R, 92C, 93B, 94R, 100T, 102B, 109T, 113R, 115T, 122R, 125R, 131C, 135R, 136B, 138L, 141T&L, 143L, 148B, 150R, 151T, 152T&B, 153T&B, 154T, 155R&B, 157L&B, 158, 160R, 162R&B, 166R, 167B, 173L, 176C&B, 178B, 179C, 182L, 185R, 186B, 190T, 193L&R, 196R, 198L&R, 199B, 200B, 201R, 203RC, 204T, 206T&B, 207R, 210T, 211R C, 212TR, 214LC, 218L, 221BL, 222B, 226R, 232T, 237T, 239B, 244L, 247B, 251R, 252B, 253B, 254B, 255B, 257B, 260T, 263T, 265R, 271R, 274, 275T, 276B, 277L, 279, 281TR, BL&BR, 282L, 284R, 285L&R, 286B, 287R, 288R, 290R, 292R&B, 293T, 301, 304R, 308L, 310T&R, 312L&R, 313T, 314L&B, 315R; **Zev Radovan/BLMJ Borowski Collection:** 15C, 84T, 179B; **Lorie Robare:** 9C, 75R, 101B, 109B; **SuperStock:** front end sheet, 8B, 9T, 10T, 12C, 13L, 14B, 26T&B, 27T, 29B, 30B, 31R, 33T, 36B, 38L, 39T&R, 40B, 42T&C, 43L, 50L, 51L, 52R, 54B, 58R, 62T, 68T, 69T&B, 71B, 72, 75B, 77T, 80L, 81C, 85L, 94L, 101C, 102T, 107T&B, 108R, 110B, 118T, 119B, 122T, 125T, 129C, 136T, 141L, 154C, 159T&B, 164T, 165T, 166B, 170T, 171T&L, 173B, 184C, 187B, 191T, 192R, 193B, 197L, 198B, 199T, 200T, 202R, 208T, 215R, 218R, 231, 232B, 233T, L&R, 235T&B, 236T, 237R, 238L, 240T, 242T&B, 243L, 246T&C, 248R, 249L&R, 251L, 253L, 258R&B, 259L&B, 261T&B, 263B, 266R&B, 267T&B, 269L&R, 270B, 271B, 272B, 296R, 299R, 303L, 307L, back end sheet.

Photo on 61B by permission of the Holy Council, St. Catherine's Monastery; James Charlesworth, Princeton Theological Seminary; and Bruce Zuckerman, West Semitic Research Project.

Special acknowledgments to the Israel Museum, Jerusalem and the Israel Antiquities Authority.

Numbers indicate pages.

T—Top	R—Right	RC—Right Center
C—Center	BR—Bottom Right	LC—Left Center
B—Bottom	TL—Top Left	LL—Lower Left
L—Left	TR—Top Right	LR—Lower Right

❧ CONTENTS ❧

INTRODUCTION • 4

ABOUT THE BIBLE • 6

LANGUAGE AND LITERATURE • 72

ANIMALS AND PLANTS • 116

TEMPLES AND SYNAGOGUES • 146

WORSHIP AND RELIGIOUS PRACTICES • 158

EVERYDAY LIFE • 194

PEOPLE AND GROUPS • 230

GEOGRAPHY • 278

INDEX • 316

❧INTRODUCTION❧

A scribe repairs a Hebrew scroll.

Though many of the stories in the Bible are well known, much of the history and background may not be as well known. Many of the events in the Bible are documented in sources other than the Bible. But how do we make the Bible come alive—make it real? *Fascinating Bible Facts* fills in the background and gives details about the people, places, and cultures of biblical times. Find out about the lives of kings and queens, emperors and warriors, and heroes and villains. These were people who breathed, ate, slept, worried, cried, and rejoiced.

To give you the best information possible, the author has chosen to quote from many sources, including the Revised Standard Version, New Revised Standard Version, King James Version, New King James Version, New American Bible, New International Version, New American Standard Version, New Jewish Publication Society Version, and the author has translated from the Hebrew. Most quotations of ancient Middle Eastern manuscripts are from *Ancient Near Eastern Texts Relating to the Old Testament*, by J. B. Pritchard.

So explore the biblical world in *Fascinating Bible Facts*. Deepen your understanding and increase your knowledge as you explore page after page!

It is not hard to imagine some of the disciples fishing in the beautiful waters of the Sea of Galilee.

✥ About the Bible ✥

Genesis: Book of Origins

The Bible's first book deals with origins, naturally enough. It tells the stories of the creation of the world and humanity. It also tells about the introduction of evil into the world. Then the book focuses upon the life of Abraham's family, the father of the Jews, through whom God established his special plans for the human race.

When Was Adam Created?

In 1650, Archbishop James Ussher calculated that the world was created in 4004 B.C. A few years later, John Lightfoot calculated that Adam was created on October 23 at 9:00 A.M. One scholar, quoted in *The Christian View of Science and Scripture*, commented dryly that "Closer than this, as a cautious scholar, the Vice-Chancellor of Cambridge University did not venture to commit himself."

Reading Backward

Often in Hebrew, words are placed out of their natural order to produce a special impact or effect. One dramatic example is in Genesis 6:9, in the phrase "Noah walked with God." Noah is found at the end of the sentence; when it is read backward, the name Enoch is revealed. Enoch was also a famous man who "walked with God" (Genesis 5:24).

Hebrew Shorthand

Rabbis interpreted some words in the Hebrew Bible as actually standing for entire phrases. That is, they argued that each letter of certain words represented a different word of a phrase. The first word of the Bible, *Br'shyt* ("in the beginning"), was said to represent several different phrases, one of which was "in the beginning God saw that Israel would accept the Torah."

Exodus: Birth of a Nation

Exodus tells the stories of Israel's captivity in Egypt and how Moses freed his people. The Ten Commandments were given on Mount Sinai, as well as details of the great Covenant Code of Laws and detailed instructions for the Tabernacle—the tent where God dwelled.

Who Was El Shaddai?

One of God's titles was *El Shaddai*, which is usually translated as "God Almighty." God told Moses that he had appeared to Abraham, Isaac, and Jacob as El Shaddai, but that he did not reveal to them the full implications of his personal name, Yahweh (Exodus 6:3).

"Moses" by Jose Ribera

The Parting of the Waters

Four times the Bible mentions waters being parted. The Red Sea parted when Israel was fleeing the Egyptians. The Jordan River parted three times, first when the Israelites under Joshua needed to cross it to enter the promised land. The second time the Jordan River parted was when Elijah and Elisha needed to cross. Later, Elisha causes the Jordan to part and he recrosses the river.

God's Hebrew name

"Moses Parts the Red Sea" by Christoffer Vilhelm Eckersberg

"I AM WHO I AM"

When Moses asked God what his name was, God responded with this cryptic phrase: "I am who I am" (Exodus 3:14). These words in Hebrew are related to God's personal name, Yahweh. God may have been revealing something profound about himself, or he also may have been reminding Moses of his earlier promise that "I will be with you" (verse 12).

God's Personal Name

Just as the Canaanite high god's personal name was Baal, the Mesopotamian high god's name was Marduk, or the Egyptian high god's name was Ra, so the Israelites' God had a personal name, Yahweh. Its exact meaning is debated; it either means "he creates" or "he is (with his people)."

Baal

Don't Say That Name!

The personal name of God (written as Y-H-W-H) was so holy to the Jews that they eventually stopped pronouncing it because they felt unworthy. When they encountered this name in the Bible while reading aloud, they substituted one of God's titles, *adonay* ("the Lord"). In most English Bibles today, God's personal name is written as "the LORD."

"Creator" by Raphael

Leviticus: Instructions for Holy Living

This book contains instructions for the Levites—the clergy for whom the book is named—and others concerning holiness. Many laws relate to animal sacrifices, but every law is related in one way or another to the need for personal holiness and blamelessness in relationship with God and with others. It contains the famous injunction about loving one's neighbor as oneself (Leviticus 19:18).

Who Was Jehovah?

Jehovah was the rendering of God's personal name that arose when the consonants of his name were combined with the vowels of its substitute in oral reading (*Y-H-W-H* and *adonay*): *Yahowah*. This mixed-up form was never heard in the Jewish synagogue, but entered the common English language by the King James Bible.

The Israelites cross the Jordan River to Canaan.

Numbers: Censuses, Laws, and Journeys

The Book of Numbers is about preparations for Israel to enter the land of Canaan. The people are numbered, more instructions are given, and the starts and stops of their journey to the promised land are detailed, including the 38 years of wandering in the wilderness.

An Ancient Folk Song

Folk songs around the world arise from everyday life, and even the Bible records some. One was sung to commemorate a well:

"Spring up, O well—sing to it—the well which the chieftains dug, which the nobles of the people started with maces, with their own staffs" (Numbers 21:17,18).

Hidden Meanings in the Numbers

In later Jewish literature, much weight was given to secret meanings hidden in the numerical values of words. In Hebrew, numbers are written using the Hebrew alphabet. Thus, in Genesis 14:14, where Abraham had 318 servants, this is seen as a hidden reference to Eliezer (the servant of Abraham, mentioned in Genesis 15:2), because 318 is the numerical value of the word Eliezer. Or, the numerical value of both the words wine and secret is 70; this led to the saying "when wine enters, secrets are out."

"Do Not Muzzle An Ox"

The Law of Moses made provision for humane treatment of animals when it stated "You shall not muzzle an ox when it treads out the grain" (Deuteronomy 25:4). The Apostle Paul saw a greater concern in that law. He used it as an allegory representing God's ministers, by which he urged the churches to generously support the clergy.

A Real Numbers Game

The finding of hidden meanings in numbers was called gematria, and it was often used to entertain and exhort, rather than to make serious claims about biblical meanings. The four consonants of God's name (Y-H-W-H) have numerical values as follows: 10, 5, 6, 5. The sum of their squares is 186, which is the numerical value of M-Q-W-M, which means "place." This reminded the rabbis that God is omnipresent (in every place).

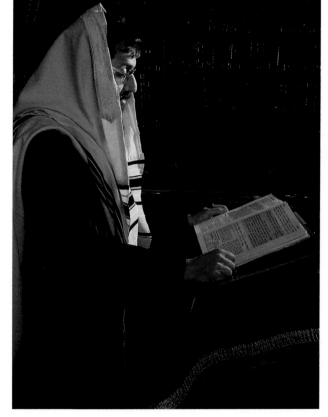

❖❖ ABOUT THE BIBLE ❖❖

The waters of the Red Sea close on the Egyptians.

Deuteronomy: Second Law

The book's title means second law, and it repeats and adds to many of the laws found in Exodus, Leviticus, and Numbers. The laws are framed by a series of Moses' last addresses to the people of Israel, in which he reviews God's gracious dealings with them in the wilderness. Moses urges the people to live faithful lives in their new land, Canaan.

The 613 Commandments

The Jewish rabbis counted 613 separate commandments in the Law of Moses. Of those, 365 of them (one for each day of the year) were stated negatively, and 248 positively. The first two of the Ten Commandments came directly from God, and 611 commandments were said to have been given through Moses. Interestingly enough, the number 611 is the numerical value of the word *Torah*, which means "law," "commandment," or "instruction."

"Moses and the Tablets" by Claude Vignon

12

The Golden Rule I

Many people know that Jesus summarized the entire Law of Moses by saying that "You shall love the Lord your God with all your heart, soul, and mind, and love your neighbor as yourself" (Matthew 22:37–40). What many don't realize is that Jesus was only quoting the Old Testament. The first command is found in Deuteronomy 6:5 and the second in Leviticus 19:18.

Jesus speaking to the crowd.

The Golden Rule II

Almost every major religion has a statement similar to Jesus' about loving one's neighbor. The great Jewish rabbi Hillel, who lived before Christ, was asked by a skeptic to teach him the entire Torah while standing on one leg. Hillel's response was, "What is hateful to yourself do not do to another. This is the whole Torah; go and study it; the rest is commentary."

"Trinity" by El Greco

Symbolic Numbers

Many numbers had symbolic value in the Bible. The number one symbolized God's unity. Three came to symbolize the Trinity. Seven was a number of completion and perfection, since God rested on the seventh day of creation. Twelve symbolized the months of the year, the tribes of Israel, and the number of apostles. Forty days or years was a common time frame in which biblical events unfolded.

Joshua

A Deadly Climax

Hebrew poetry can be very dramatic. The poetic description of Sisera's (the Canaanite general) death, whom Jael killed with a tent peg through his temple, shows an awful death struggle:
"Between her feet he sank, he fell, he lay,
Between her feet he sank, he fell.
Where he sank, there he fell,
Dead" (Judges 5:27).

Joshua: Book of the Land

This book focuses entirely on the land of Canaan and the Israelites' possession of it as the fulfillment of God's promise to Abraham. Moses' successor, Joshua, led Israel into the land, did battle with the Canaanites at Jericho and elsewhere, and portioned out the land to the 12 tribes of Israel.

"Creation of Man" by Michelangelo

Hallelu–Yah!

The word *hallelujah* is Hebrew for "praise the Lord." It contains a shortened form of God's name: Yah (for Yahweh). Many biblical characters' names end similarly: Hezekiah is *chizqi-yah* "Yahweh is my strength," and Isaiah is *yesha-yahu* "Yahweh saves."

❧ ABOUT THE BIBLE ❧

Elohim: God or gods?

Elohim is the Hebrew word for "God" and it also is the word for (foreign) "gods." It is a grammatically plural word (it means gods), but when it refers to God, it takes a singular verb. This plural form of the word for one God is sometimes called the plural of majesty. It is almost as if God's attributes are so many and he is so great that no mere singular noun can do him justice.

Household gods

Large Symbolic Numbers

Many significant numbers were multiples of smaller symbolic numbers. Seventy was a large number of completion. The number 666 is the mark of the beast in Revelation 13:18, a symbol of the antichrist. The number 1,000 symbolized something indefinitely large. The number 144,000 is the number of saints sealed up to God in Revelation 7:4 and 14:1.

Judges: Time of Turmoil

The book of Israel's judges tells a story of a repeated cycle of the nation's sin, enslavement, and deliverance by warrior-judges. The cycle spirals downward, however, and by the end of the book things are so bad that the author despairingly says, "in those days there was no king in Israel; everyone did what was right in their own eyes."

The Lion and the Bees

Riddles were common in the biblical world. Their intent was to puzzle the hearers. Only after the riddle was interpreted did its point become clear. A well-known riddle was Samson's: "Out of the eater came something to eat. Out of the strong came something sweet" (Judges 14:14). This referred to a lion he had killed and in whose carcass bees had made honey. Because the riddle was answered, Samson killed 30 Philistines with the jawbone of an ass.

Whatever in the World Is Onomatopoeia?!

This refers to words that sound like what they describe, such as "buzz" or "boom." An interesting Hebrew example refers to the "galloping, galloping" sounds of Canaanite warhorses in an Israelite victory song: *"daharote, daharote"* (Judges 5:22).

15

Ruth: Exemplar of the Virtuous Woman

In the Hebrew Bible, the Book of Ruth immediately follows the Book of Proverbs (rather than the Book of Judges, as it does in the Christian canon). This is probably because Proverbs ends with the great poem about the many virtues of a godly woman (Proverbs 31:10–31). The Book of Ruth follows because Ruth is a perfect example of just such a woman.

Boaz asks about Ruth.

Ruth: A Love Story

The Book of Ruth is a literary masterpiece, a sparkling gem that tells a heartwarming story about a widowed woman (Naomi) and her daughter-in-law (Ruth) for whom things finally work out in the end. Ruth marries Boaz, who provides for them both. The family tree at the book's end connects Ruth with Abraham and shows her to be David's great-grandmother.

Samuel anoints David.

1 and 2 Samuel: King David's Story

These books tell of the introduction of kingship in Israel under the prophet Samuel. Israel's first king, Saul, was disqualified, and David became king. Three-quarters of the book is devoted to David's rise to power and to his reign. God promised David an unbroken line of successors on the throne of the kingdom.

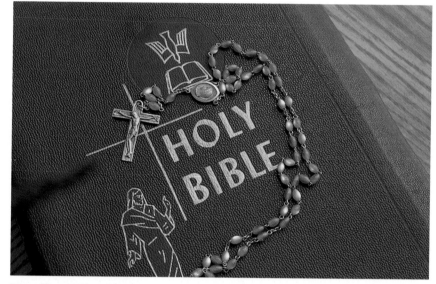

Copyists' Misteaks (sic)

Scholars who believe the Bible was originally written without any errors do not argue that there were no mistakes in its copying. As manuscripts were copied again and again by hand over many centuries, many misspellings, additions, and omissions occurred. Fortunately, enough biblical manuscripts survive so scholars can compare them and confidently judge what the original texts say.

Medieval Copyists

During the Middle Ages, Jewish scribes and Christian monks kept the Scriptures alive by laboriously copying them over and over again by hand. Copying became a true art form. Jewish scribes and monks, for example, used elaborate calligraphy and different-colored inks in their manuscripts. They also drew tiny, beautifully detailed pictures in the margins and at the beginning of chapters.

Dueling Versions?

Bible translators must resort to educated guesses in those rare instances where the texts we have are unintelligible. In 1 Samuel 13:1, the King James Version reads: "Saul reigned one year; and when he had reigned two years...." The New American Standard Version reads "Saul was forty years old when he began to reign, and he reigned thirty-two years...." The New International Version reads "Saul was thirty years old when he became king, and he reigned forty-two years...."

Was Saul An Infant King?

A famous text where copying errors have crept in is in 1 Samuel 13:1. The Hebrew literally reads "Saul was one year old when he became king, and he reigned two years over Israel." Since we know that Saul became king as an adult and that he reigned for more than two years, this indicates that at least two numbers were missed by an ancient copyist.

Temple scroll from Qumran

A Reverence for Scripture

In early Jewish custom, translation of the Hebrew Scriptures in the worship services could only be done orally, not read from a scroll. This probably was to preserve the distinctiveness and sacredness of the written Hebrew Scriptures. It is said of the great Rabbi Gamaliel, the Apostle Paul's teacher, that he rejected a written copy of the Aramaic Targum of Job and had it buried in a wall.

1 and 2 Kings: The Kings of Israel and Judah

Under David's son Solomon, the nation began to crumble and eventually it split into two: northern Israel (ten tribes) and southern Judah (two tribes). These books chronicle the fortunes of the two kingdoms. Israel had an unbroken succession of bad kings and Judah had the descendants of David and a mixture of good and bad kings. The books end with Israel annihilated and Judah under Babylonian captivity.

The Septuagint

The earliest Greek translation of the Hebrew Bible is called the Septuagint. Supposedly, 72 translators (representing six from each tribe of Israel) were convened in Alexandria, Egypt, about 250 B.C., but scholars today put its translation later, and taking place over a long period of time. This translation was needed because so many Jews throughout the Mediterranean world only spoke Greek.

Aramaic Targums

Aramaic was a sister language to Hebrew, and was used starting in the late Old Testament period. The earliest Aramaic translations of the Hebrew Bible were the Targums. These were oral paraphrases on each book, not exact translations, and they were laden with commentary and explanatory glosses. The earliest of these were committed to writing during the period between the composition of the last book of the Old Testament and the first book of the New Testament.

18

⁂ ABOUT THE BIBLE ⁂

The Hebrew Bible: Different Ordering

Even though it has the same books as the Christian Old Testament, the Hebrew Bible arranges its contents differently. It has three sections, called (in order) the Law, the Prophets, and the Writings. The Prophets include the historical books such as 1 and 2 Samuel along with the traditional prophets, such as Isaiah. The Writings include Psalms and many other miscellaneous books, and it ends with 2 Chronicles.

King David

1 and 2 Chronicles: David's Kingdom

Fully half of these two books are copied word-for-word from 1 and 2 Samuel and 1 and 2 Kings, but the author presents a very different slant. He is only interested in the fortunes of David and the kingdom of Judah (which represented David's descendants), and he consistently evaluates the nation's fortunes in terms of its trust in God.

Books that Defile the Hands

For Jewish rabbis, books that were given by divine inspiration were ones that "defiled the hands" if they were touched. This idea prevented irreverent use of the Scriptures. If people had to wash their hands every time they handled the Scriptures, they would do so carefully and reverently.

The Hebrew Bible: Different Numbering

Early references to the Hebrew Bible (the Old Testament) mentioned only 22 or 24 books in it, instead of 39, as found in Christian Bibles, even though their contents are identical. This is because books such as 1 and 2 Kings were counted as one, and the 12 minor prophets (Hosea through Malachi) were counted as one, called the Book of the Twelve.

Solomon's Temple

Ezra and Nehemiah: Books of Restoration

These books show the restoration of Judah after the destruction of Jerusalem and its exile in Babylon. The Temple was rebuilt and Ezra and Nehemiah returned from exile to Judah to start religious and political reforms, which included rebuilding the walls of the city.

Selective Genealogies

The Bible has many genealogies, listing generation after generation almost endlessly, it seems at times. Sometimes these genealogies are not all-inclusive, however. Jesus is called "the son of David, the son of Abraham" (Matthew 1:1), when obviously many generations separated the three men. A list of Aaron's descendants in Ezra 7:1–5 omits six people who are found in the parallel list in 1 Chronicles 6:3–14.

Jesus

Esther: God's Protection in Exile

The Book of Esther tells of the fortunes of a Jewish family who never returned from exile, but who flourished in a foreign land. Esther and her uncle Mordechai were favored and rose in the Persian court, despite strong opposition, and they were able to avert a great slaughter of Jews.

"Queen Esther" by Andrea del Castagno

Esther confronts the king about Haman.

Esther: Book of Controversy

The Book of Esther has provoked strong reactions. Negatively, Martin Luther, the great Protestant reformer, wrote that "I am so hostile to this book [2 Maccabees] and to Esther that I could wish they did not exist at all." Positively, Maimonides, the great Jewish rabbi, elevated it to near equality with the Law of Moses, saying that the Law and Esther would still stand after all other Scripture had perished.

"Job" by Leon Bonnat

Job: Questions About Innocent Suffering

The Book of Job is one of the world's classics on the question of human suffering and divine justice. Job, an innocent man who feared God, is put through much suffering. Through this, Job passionately questions God but he never abandons belief in God. After a direct encounter with God, Job's questions cease and his fortunes are fully restored.

Job

What is Wisdom?

Wisdom in the biblical sense refers to knowing how to live life well, in all its dimensions, including relationships with God and with one's fellow human beings. The three "wisdom" books in the Bible are Job, Proverbs, and Ecclesiastes. The Book of Proverbs begins by stating that "The fear of the Lord is the beginning of knowledge; fools despise wisdom and instruction" (Proverbs 1:7).

❧ ABOUT THE BIBLE ❧

How Can Wisdom Be Acquired?

Job 28 contains a majestic poem reflecting on what wisdom is and how it can be acquired. It states that wisdom is not to be found in the deepest sea, nor can it be bought for gold, nor can any animal or human being know it on its own. Only "God understands the way to it, and he knows its place" (verse 23). God reveals wisdom to humans.

Two-in-One Psalms

Some psalms now separated in the Bible originally were part of one composition. Psalms 9 and 10 contain an acrostic poem that begins with the first letter of the Hebrew alphabet in Psalm 9:1 and ends in Psalm 10:17 with the last letter. Psalms 42 and 43 share a common refrain, also showing a common origin.

"I've Told You a Million Times Not to Exaggerate!"

Hyperbole, or exaggeration, is a common poetic device in Hebrew. In describing his troubles, one psalmist says "I am sinking in deep slime...I have come into deep water, and the flood sweeps me away" (Psalm 69:1). It is comical to imagine the poet literally holding scroll and pen above the water as he sinks out of sight!

Psalms: Israel's Songs and Prayers

The 150 psalms in the Psalter formed a hymn book of sorts for Israel. These hymns cover the range of human emotion, from ecstatic joy to deepest despair. They have taught Jews and Christians how to sing and pray, and also convey truths about God and everyday faith and life.

King David mosaic

Duplicate Psalms

Some psalms appear more than once in the Bible. David's song of praise when God delivered him from the hands of Saul appears as 2 Samuel 22 and also as Psalm 18. The psalm beginning "The fool says in his heart, 'There is no God,'" appears as both Psalm 14 and 53.

Ark of the Covenant

Cut-and-Paste Psalms

Some psalms were composed in much the same way that modern church prayer books are, by stringing together different portions of Scripture to form new compositions. Psalm 108 is made up entirely of parts of Psalms 57 and 60, and the lengthy hymn of thanksgiving when the Ark reached Jerusalem found in 1 Chronicles 16 is composed of poetry found in three psalms: 96, 105, and 106.

Head for the Center

A well-written essay usually states its objective somewhere near the beginning. Some biblical psalms, however, make their main point halfway through. These psalms are so precisely constructed that you can count the number of Hebrew words in the psalm, divide by two, and find the psalm's most important thought precisely at the midpoint. Examples include Psalms 8, 23, 95, and 100.

23

Which Psalm Is It?

Protestant Bibles (which follow the Hebrew Bible's numbering system) number the psalms differently from many Roman Catholic and Orthodox Bibles (which follow the earliest Greek and Latin versions). In the latter, Psalms 9 and 10 were treated as one psalm. Thus, the numbering of Psalms 10 through 113 is off by one. After this, several other adjustments in how psalms are divided also affect the numbering. All Bibles end with 150 total psalms, however.

Psalm Titles

Many of the psalms (116 in all) have titles that were added in antiquity. Many attribute the psalm to a certain author (David, Asaph, sons of Korah), while many classify the psalm (as a prayer, a praise, a *maskil*, a *miktam*, a *shiggaion*). Some contain musical instructions ("For the choir director"), while others have historical notes ("A Psalm of David, when Nathan the prophet came to him after he went into Bathsheba").

Books Within the Psalter

The Book of Psalms is organized into five books, consisting of Psalms 1 to 41, 42 to 72, 73 to 89, 90 to 106, and 107 to 150. Each of these concludes with a short doxology, praising God, and the word amen. The Jewish Midrash (commentary) on the Psalms, written in the tenth century A.D., equates this division with that of the Pentateuch: "As Moses gave five books of laws to Israel, so David gave five books of Psalms to Israel."

Moses

Steps to Herod's Temple

Psalms Outside the Psalter

Besides the 150 psalms in the biblical Psalter, the Bible has many other psalms scattered throughout other books. Famous examples include psalms in Exodus 15 (Moses and Miriam's Song of the Sea), Deuteronomy 32 (Moses' song), Judges 5 (Deborah and Barak's victory song), 1 Samuel 2 (Hannah's song of praise), 2 Samuel 1 (David's lament), Jonah 2 (Jonah's prayer of thanksgiving), Habakkuk 3 (Habakkuk's song of praise), and Luke 1 (Mary's song of praise, sometimes called The Magnificat).

The angel visits Mary.

Psalms for a Pilgrimage

Fifteen consecutive psalms have the title "A Psalm of Ascents": Psalms 120 to 134. Rabbinic tradition states that there were 15 steps going up from the Women's Court in the Temple to the Israelites' Court, and that a psalm was composed for each. More likely, these psalms were composed for the pilgrimage up to Jerusalem, "the mountain of the Lord" (Isaiah 30:29).

Biblical Acrostics

Highly structured Hebrew poetry found its most specialized expression in the acrostic poem, where each succeeding verse in the poem began with succeeding letters of the Hebrew alphabet, 22 in all. Psalms 25, 34, 37, 111, 112, 119, and 145 are all examples of this. The poem extolling the virtues of a godly woman in Proverbs 31:10–31 is also an acrostic.

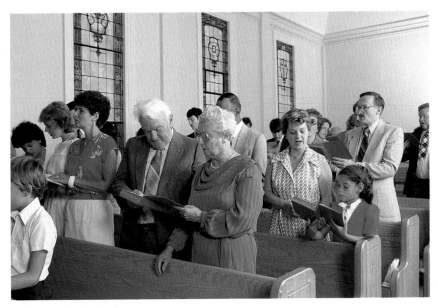

Name That Tune!

Many psalm titles contain musical instructions that are not clear today. These include Psalm 6 ("According to the Sheminith"), Psalm 22 ("According to 'The Hind of the Dawn'"), Psalm 45 ("According to 'Lilies'"), and Psalm 56 ("According to 'The Dove on Far-Off Terebinths'"). These probably refer to the titles of specific tunes to be used with these psalms.

"God Creating the Earth" by Raphael

Who is Lady Wisdom?

In Proverbs 8, wisdom is personified as a woman. It tells of her attributes and her creation by God. She says "By me kings reign, and rulers decree what is just.... I love those who love me, and those who seek me diligently find me.... The Lord created me at the beginning of his work, the first of his acts of old."

The Lady and the Harlot

The author of Proverbs uses a vivid contrast to make a point about right living. He urges his son in chapter 7 to reject the "loose woman," the "harlot, wily of heart," warning him in detail of the dangers of the seductive call of the harlot who looks out of her window. Instead, the young man is urged to let himself be seduced by "Lady Wisdom" (chapter 8): "Does not wisdom call, does not understanding raise her voice?"

Ecclesiastes: The Worldly Wise Preacher

The Book of Ecclesiastes is written by someone who has tried everything in search for meaning in life, but who has come up empty. It is full of frustration, even cynicism, but the book ends by affirming that life has meaning when lived in right relation with God. It is the closest piece of writing in the Bible to what the Greeks called philosophy.

Proverbs: Practical Wisdom

This book is one of the most practical books in the Bible, with its common-sense approach to life. This is captured in hundreds of short, pithy sayings (proverbs) about how to live life well, in all its dimensions, with God and our neighbors.

Wherever in the World Is Lady Wisdom?

Any computer game searching for Lady Wisdom would have to look at the 24th chapter of the apocryphal Book of Sirach. Here too wisdom is a woman, and she states that the Creator assigned her to "make your dwelling in...Israel.... I took root in an honored people" (Sirach 24:8,12). The key to wisdom, according to this chapter, is "the book of the covenant of the Most High God, the law that Moses commanded us."

Solomon: A Real Numbers Cruncher

The Book of Proverbs contains many proverbs of Solomon, including one section entitled "The Proverbs of Solomon" (Solomon 10:1–22:16). In this section there are exactly 375 proverbs. Not coincidentally, 375 is the numerical value of Solomon's name.

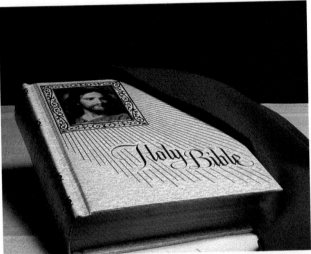

Phantom Books

The Bible often refers to books that no longer exist. In the Old Testament, these include the Book of Jashar, the Book of the Wars of the Lord, the Chronicles of King David, and the Commentary of Iddo the Seer. In the New Testament, the Book of Enoch is mentioned, and several passages quote from other documents without naming them.

Song of Solomon: Love Songs

This book, also called the Song of Songs, is a beautiful collection of love poetry, much of which is rather explicit, even erotic. Some Jews and Christians have seen in the book a description of God's relationship with Israel or the Christian Church, and thereby avoided some of their embarrassment about the language of love.

Detail of "Esther and Mordechai" by Aert de Gelder

Where is God?

Two books in the Bible do not mention God even once: the Song of Solomon, which is a collection of love poetry, and the Book of Esther, which tells of the Jewish people's life and successes under Persian rule.

Songs

Drinking songs are part of almost every culture, and the prophets Amos and Isaiah disapprovingly referred to them in biblical society. Isaiah even quotes two such songs: "Let us eat and drink, for tomorrow we die" (Isaiah 22:13). "'Come,' they say, 'let us get wine, let us fill ourselves with strong drink. And tomorrow will be like today, great beyond measure'" (Isaiah 56:12).

Playing With Words

Hebrew writers often used words that sounded similar to illustrate their ideas. The prophet Isaiah made an effective point about conditions in the land with the following word play:
"And God looked for justice (*mishpat*),
but he only found bloodshed (*mishpach*);
he looked for righteousness (*tsedaqah*),
but he only found a cry of distress (*tse`aqah*)!"
(Isaiah 5:7).

A Children's Ditty

The drunken prophets mocked Isaiah, comparing his words to a meaningless children's ditty:
"Do and do, do and do,
rule on rule, rule on rule,
a little here, a little there"
(Isaiah 28:10).

"Children on Beach" by E. Polthast

Isaiah: Prophet Par Excellence

The Book of Isaiah is arguably the greatest of the prophetic books. Its scope is all-encompassing. The book ranges from dramatic excoriations of wicked Judah to tender assurances of God's love and restoration to visions of the new heavens and the new earth. Many passages from Handel's *Messiah* are taken from Isaiah.

Jerusalem

"The Sixth Sick Sheik's Sixth Sheep's Sick"

The Hebrew language may not have any tongue-twisters quite this difficult, but the use of assonance (successive words containing the same sounds) is common. One psalmist soothingly says, *"sha'alu shelom yerushalayim"* ("Pray for the peace of Jerusalem," Psalm 122:6). Isaiah packs a powerful punch by preaching that *"pachad wapachat wapach"* ("terror and pit and snare") will come upon the wicked (Isaiah 24:17).

What Was That Reference Again?

The New Testament often quotes from the Old Testament. However, sometimes it is not clear which passage is in view, as when Matthew quoted "He [Jesus] shall be called a Nazarene" (Matthew 2:23). Jesus was from Nazareth, but no such prophecy is found in the Old Testament. It may be a wordplay from Isaiah 11:1, a Messianic prophecy referring to the "branch" (Hebrew *nezer*).

Nazareth

"Jeremiah" by Michelangelo

Jeremiah and Lamentations: Books of Passion

The prophet Jeremiah revealed his personal passions more than any other prophet. He wept bitterly over the sins of his people, and argued bitterly with God for sending him as a prophet. He was vigorously opposed by false priests and prophets, and suffered much for his stand. The Book of Lamentations contains five passionate laments over the destruction of Jerusalem, traditionally ascribed to Jeremiah.

EZECHIEL

Ezekiel: Prophet in Exile

Ezekiel's book contains many strange visions and strange actions. His message was to the Jews in Babylonian exile, helping them to make sense of their punishment and pointing them to a way of restoration. Along with Jeremiah, he emphasized the concept of each individual's responsibility for his or her own sin, a concept that had been forgotten in Judah. His book ends with a great vision of the ideal temple.

Lamentations and Acrostics

Perhaps the most emotional book in the Bible is the Book of Lamentations, which has five chapters of anguished laments over the destruction of Jerusalem. Strangely, these heart-felt laments are expressed in the rigid structure of the acrostic: each chapter has 22 verses (or a multiple of 22).

"Vision of Ezekiel" by Raphael

Apocalyptic Literature

This is a type of Jewish and early Christian literature that mostly dates from 200 B.C. to A.D. 100. It is rich with symbolism, angels, and other spiritual beings; it communicates through dreams and visions; and it is often very difficult to interpret precisely. A major topic it addresses is the end of time. In the Bible, the major apocalyptic portions are Ezekiel 40 through 48, Daniel 7 through 12, Zechariah 9 through 14, and the Book of Revelation.

A Hebrew Cryptogram

A fascinating literary device found occasionally in the Hebrew Bible is called *atbash*. It created code words by substituting the first letter of the alphabet for the last, the second for the next-to-last, and so on. A famous example is in Jeremiah 51:41, where Sheshach is a cryptogram for Babylon.

Faces and Wheels

Ezekiel had a glittering vision about four shining manlike creatures that were accompanied by four wheels (Ezekiel 1). The creatures each had four wings and four faces. The faces were those of a man, a lion, an ox, and an eagle. The wheels did not turn, but they had eyes in them, and they flew wherever the creatures flew. The vision portrayed God's majesty in vivid terms.

Daniel: Visionary Prophet

The Book of Daniel contains an equal mixture of stories about Daniel and his friends in exile—such as Daniel in the lions' den or his three friends (Shadrach, Meshach, and Abednego) in the fiery furnace—and of visions about the future. The common thread between both parts of the book is the idea of God's control of the world's empires and his vindication of his people.

Daniel in the lions' den

A Censored Chapter

The first chapter of the Book of Ezekiel may have portrayed God's majesty, but it was very strange. In fact, it was so difficult and so strange that Jewish young people under 30 years old were not allowed to read it!

Can You Keep A Secret?

The Book of Daniel contains explicit words about the book's focus: Much of it was not for the present, but for a future time. Daniel was instructed in a vision to "seal up the vision, for it pertains to many days hence" (Daniel 8:26) and to "shut up the words, and seal the book, until the time of the end" (Daniel 12:4).

"Belshazzar Sees the Writing on the Wall" by Rembrandt

The Handwriting on the Wall

This common expression traces its origin to the Book of Daniel, when the Babylonian king Belshazzar was giving a great feast. We are told that a great hand appeared and began writing on the wall. The message was one of doom for this king, who was persecuting the Jews, and he died that very night.

Hosea: Israel's Adultery

God told Hosea to marry a prostitute, and so he had to suffer her unfaithfulness. All of this was a metaphor for Israel's adultery against God when Israel followed other gods. The book speaks eloquently about Israel worshiping other gods and its neglect of social concerns.

An Aramaic Puzzle

The prophet Daniel was able to interpret the handwriting on the wall of King Belshazzar's palace. The words were *mene, mene, tekel, parsin,* which mean "numbered, weighed, divided." This signified that Belshazzar's days were numbered, that he had been weighed in the balance and found wanting, and that his kingdom would be divided among the Persians (whose name is a word play on *parsin*).

Canaanite goddess Ashtoreth

33

Amos: Israel's Social Conscience

More than any prophet, Amos spoke out against social evils, such as abuse of power, oppression of the poor, dishonest dealings, and insincere religious ritual. He even spoke out against the life of leisure, and the many possessions and the summer homes of the wealthy. These luxuries blinded the people to the very real needs around them.

Amos

Joel: The Day of the Lord

This short book focuses on the concept of the "Day of the Lord." This sometimes refers to God's immediate judgment on nations that oppressed others (such as in a great locust plague), and sometimes refers to God's judgment of all nations at the end of time. The Apostle Peter quoted extensively from Joel 2 (see Acts 2), applying its prophecies to his own day.

Obadiah: Edom's Doom

This shortest book in the Old Testament is a brief but concentrated blast of condemnation at Judah's neighbor Edom, located southeast of the Dead Sea. Edom had rejoiced at Jerusalem's downfall, and this book speaks about that.

A Pun-ishing Experience

Speakers of Hebrew loved a good pun. The prophet Amos was once shown a vision of a basket of "(ripe) summer fruit" (Hebrew *qayits*), to illustrate the point that the "end" (Hebrew *qets*) had come for Israel—the time was "ripe" for destruction (Amos 8:2).

Jonah: Prophet to Assyria

The message of this little jewel is often obscured by discussions about the fish that swallowed Jonah. It is a wonderful book about God's concern for all people, not just his chosen people. Jonah was sent to Nineveh, the capital of the world's largest empire, to urge its people to repent, and they did.

> ### Word-Links in the Bible
> Sometimes word-links between adjacent books of the Bible can be seen, which probably accounts for their being placed together. The following phrase occurs near the end of the Book of Joel (Joel 3:16): "The Lord roars from Zion, and sends forth his voice from Jerusalem." The next book, Amos, begins with exactly the same phrase (Amos 1:2).

Jonah cast into the sea.

Chronology and the Order of the Bible's Books

In the Old Testament, the first 17 books (Genesis through Esther) are in essentially chronological order, beginning with creation and ending with the Jews in exile at the end of the Old Testament period. Other books are not grouped chronologically. The prophetic books are arranged with the three longest books first. Most of the prophets fit chronologically into the time period covered by the books of 1 and 2 Kings.

Bethlehem

Micah: Typical Prophet

Micah fits well the stereotype of a biblical prophet, speaking out against both social and spiritual evils, and also looking into the future and speaking of the restoration of God's people. He predicted that the Messiah would come from Bethlehem, and he summarized well the duties of God's people: "And what does the Lord require of you but to do justice, and to love kindness, and to walk humbly with your God?" (Micah 6:8).

"Prophet" by Donatello

Nahum and Zephaniah: Angry Prophets

These two minor prophets had short, intense messages. Nahum's was a quick, sustained blast of fury against Nineveh, the capital of the oppressive Assyrian Empire. Zephaniah's was a blast of judgment on Judah, Jerusalem, and Judah's enemies, followed by promises of salvation.

Habakkuk: Questioning God

This wonderful little book, hidden away among the other minor prophets, questions why God would allow evil to run rampant. It is similar to Job (both are known as theodicies, books that question God's justice). God's answer is that his justice always prevails, even if it takes time. The book ends with a psalm that speaks joyfully of an encounter with God.

Jeremiah

The Arrangement of the Prophetic Books

The longest prophetic books come first (Isaiah, Jeremiah, Ezekiel), the major prophets, and the 12 minor prophets follow. A rough (but not exact) chronological order can be seen here, since Hosea and Amos were the earliest and they appear first, and Haggai, Zechariah, and Malachi, the later prophets, appear last.

Haggai and Zechariah: Prophets of the Temple

Haggai and Zechariah both had messages for the community that had returned to Jerusalem after exile in Babylon. Haggai wrote about the rebuilding of the Temple, and Zechariah about the Temple and the future. Zechariah predicted the coming of Jerusalem's future king riding on a donkey, which Jesus did when he rode into Jerusalem the week before his death (celebrated by Christians as Palm Sunday).

"Christ's Triumphant Entrance Into Jerusalem" by Bernard Plockhorst

36

Malachi: The Last Prophet

Malachi spoke about the abysmal conditions that existed after the Jews had settled and become complacent in their land once again. This included the corruption and neglect of the priesthood and the neglect of giving to God. His book ends with a prediction of the prophet Elijah's return, which the Book of Matthew applies to John the Baptist.

Malachi

The "Hidden Books" Called the Apocrypha

The word *apocrypha* means "hidden," and it usually refers to 12 or more books added to the 39 books of the Hebrew Bible. These were written between 200 B.C. and A.D. 100, and are considered by many Christians to be part of the Bible since most were found in the first Greek translations of the Hebrew Bible. The Roman Catholic Church accepts 12 additional books, while Eastern Orthodox Churches accept 4 to 5 books beyond that.

Tobit and Judith: Two Literary Masterpieces

Tobit and Sarah are the two righteous heroes of the Book of Tobit, both of whom are helped by the angel Raphael. Tobit was healed of blindness and Sarah was rid of a demon. Tobit is one of the most popular books of the Apocrypha. Judith is also a literary masterpiece. It tells of the Assyrian general Holofernes' war against the Jews and of the beautiful widow Judith's deadly trickery.

"Judith and Holofernes" by Artemisia Gentileschi

"The Sacrifice of Isaac" by Giovanni Battista Gaulli

The Additions to Esther: Restoring God

The Greek translation of the Book of Esther has six substantial additions, which add 107 verses to the 167 verses of the Hebrew text. Their purpose is to give a clearly religious slant to the book. The extra verses make frequent reference to God, they emphasize his choice of Abraham and Israel, and they talk about prayer. The Book of Esther mentions none of these.

Jeremiah dictates to Baruch.

Wisdom of Solomon and Sirach: Books of the Sages

These two Apocryphal books are "wisdom" books in the tradition of the Book of Proverbs. Their subject matter ranges from practical advice in everyday living to mature philosophical reflections on the nature of wisdom itself. The Wisdom of Sirach is also known as Ecclesiasticus.

Solomon

Baruch and the Letter of Jeremiah: Help for Hard Times

Baruch was Jeremiah's secretary, and this book is supposed to be from him. It consists of confessions of Israel's guilt after the fall of Jerusalem, and two poems on wisdom and comfort in hard times. The Letter of Jeremiah is presented as Jeremiah's words to his followers. The letter expands on the thought in Jeremiah 10:11, which speaks of the reality of God and the unreality of idols.

"The Suicide of Saul" by Brueghel the Elder

The Book of Jashar

The Bible twice quotes from a book it calls the Book of Jashar (or the Book of the Upright One). The incident when the sun and moon stood still in Joshua's day is said to have been recorded in this book (Joshua 10:13), as is David's lament over the deaths of Saul and Jonathan (2 Samuel 1:18). The book has not survived, however, although a late Jewish book of that title was written in an attempt to reproduce it.

The Additions to Daniel: Entertaining Stories

Three Apocryphal books contain additional stories about the prophet Daniel. The Song of the Three Jews contains prayers and hymns of Daniel's three friends who were thrown into the fiery furnace. The Book of Susanna tells of Daniel's rescue of Susanna, a woman who had been wronged. Bel and the Dragon tells two highly entertaining satirical tales that ridicule idolatry.

Model of Solomon's Temple

1 and 2 Maccabees: Intertestamental History

These two lengthy books focus on the fortunes of the Jews from about 175 to 132 B.C. They tell of the Jews' revolt against intolerant Syrian rule, the Syrians' desecration of the Temple and the Jews' recapture of Jerusalem and the Temple under Judas Maccabeus. They end with the establishment of Judea as an independent state.

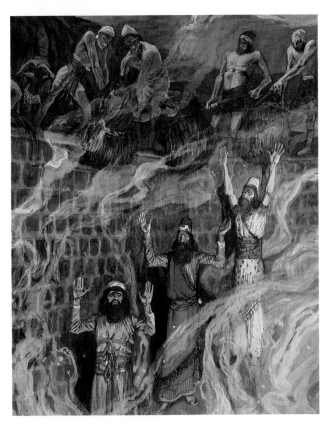
"In the Fiery Furnace" by James J. Tissot

39

Hunting for the Nativity

The most popular Christian holiday is Christmas, and yet the well-known and much-beloved Christmas stories of Jesus' birth are found only two places in the Bible: Matthew 1 and 2, and Luke 1 and 2. Mark and John, both gospels about Jesus' life, don't even mention these wonderful stories.

Was Jesus Born "Before Christ"?

Jesus was born some time around the year 6 B.C. King Herod, who attempted to kill baby Jesus by killing all the Jewish male infants in and around Bethlehem, died in 4 B.C. This discrepancy is owed to the monk Dennis the Little, who in A.D. 532 came up with the idea of marking years starting with Christ's birth. Unfortunately, the year of his birth was not known until much more recently.

"The Nativity" by Beato Angelico

Matthew: A Jewish Gospel

The Book of Matthew was written primarily for a Jewish audience. The book shows that Jesus was the Jewish Messiah, a king, and that he was descended from David and Abraham. Matthew records the story of the wise men visiting the baby Jesus, an event fitting for a king. Luke records the humbler story of the shepherds visiting Jesus.

"Adoration of the Shepherds" by Guido Reni

Which Day Is Jesus' Birthday?

December 25 was celebrated as the birth date of Jesus by the early fourth century A.D., and probably much earlier. This date was probably selected because the Romans celebrated the Mithraic festival of the sun god on that day, and this was an opportunity to make a pagan festival into a religious one. This date was also near the winter solstice. The Eastern Church celebrates Christmas on January 6. The exact date of Jesus' birth is unknown.

How Many Wise Men?

Tradition has it that three wise men came from the East to visit the baby Jesus. Traditionally, their names were Melchior, Gaspar, and Balthasar. In fact, the Gospel of Matthew mentions neither their names nor how many they were. The number three arose from the gifts of gold, frankincense, and myrrh that they brought.

Who Were the Magi?

The Greek historian Herodotus (fifth century B.C.) spoke of magi who were a priestly tribe in the Persian empire. Later (in the Book of Acts), the term refers to anyone who practiced magic arts (the word "magic" comes from *magi*). The most famous magi were the wise men who visited the baby Jesus. Matthew states that they came to Bethlehem from the East; tradition has located this in Persia, Babylonia, or Arabia.

The Star in the East

The nature of the famous star that guided the wise men has remained elusive. Scientific suggestions have included a comet, a new star, a supernova, the planet Venus, or a convergence of several planets. A comet was recorded about 4 B.C., and Jupiter, Mars, and Saturn converged in the constellation Pisces in 6 B.C. Both of these events could fit the biblical story.

"Adoration of the Magi" by Perugino

"The Rising of Lazarus" by Fra Angelico

Mark: An Action-Packed Gospel

Mark's account of Jesus' life is the shortest and the most action-oriented. Mark portrays Jesus as one who was constantly serving others. Mark records 18 miracles and only 4 full parables. In contrast, a much greater emphasis on Jesus' teachings is in the other gospels.

Luke: Beloved Physician's Gospel

Luke was the only Gentile among the New Testament's authors, and he wrote for a Gentile audience. As a medical doctor, he tells us that he investigated his subject matter thoroughly before setting forth his account (Luke 1:1–4), and his eye for details is evident. His book also has a warm, human touch to it.

Extended Parables

Many of Jesus' parables were stories. they involved comparisons, and the characters often represented God the Father or Jesus himself. Among the most beloved extended parables are the shepherd who risks all to search for his one lost sheep, the father who eagerly takes back his long-wayward son, and the good Samaritan who stopped to help a robbery victim when members of society's elite would not.

"The Pharisees Question Jesus" by James J. Tissot

Jesus' Blasphemy?

In the course of a debate with a group of Jews, Jesus claimed to have seen Abraham. When they challenged this statement, he replied, "before Abraham was, I am" (John 8:58). The Jews were enraged with this reference to "I am," since only God was to be referred to in this way. They considered this blasphemy, and tried to stone Jesus to death. This is one of the most direct statements in the Gospels equating Jesus with God.

The Parables of Jesus

Jesus' favorite teaching tool was the parable. In its simplest form, the parable uses a comparison to make a point. It is simple, direct, and the point is clear, such as "The kingdom of heaven is like treasure hidden in a field, which someone found and hid; then in his joy he goes and sells all that he has and buys that field" (Matthew 13:44).

The Eye of a Needle

Jesus used hyperbole when he said, "It is easier for a camel to go through the eye of a needle than for a rich man to enter the kingdom of God" (Mark 10:25). An unfounded tradition that this referred to a small pedestrian gate in the center of Jerusalem's wooden gates arose in the Middle Ages to soften the import of this proverb.

John: A Theological Gospel

The Apostle John's picture of Jesus is the most theological of the four Gospels. His focus is upon Jesus as the Son of God the Father. His book is addressed to the world at large, and his purpose was to convince people that Jesus was the Messiah, the Son of God (John 20:31). The action is slower than in Mark's Gospel, with more attention to conversations and teaching.

"Jesus and the Children" by Hugo Vogel

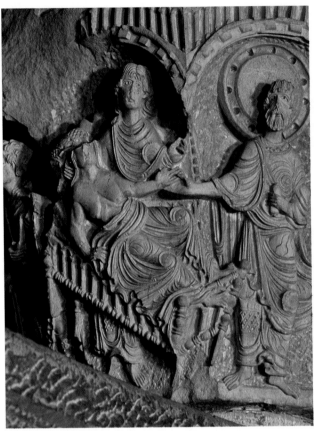

The Raising of Tabitha

Resurrection from the Dead

The Bible tells of many people coming back to life after having been dead. In the Old Testament, a widow's son was brought back to life by Elijah (1 Kings 17); the son of a wealthy couple was raised by Elisha (2 Kings 4); and a man whose corpse was thrown into Elisha's grave came back to life (2 Kings 13). In the New Testament, a widow's son (Luke 7), Jairus's daughter (Luke 8), and Lazarus (John 11) were raised by Jesus. Dorcas (also known as Tabitha) was brought back to life by Peter (Acts 9). Paul brought back Eutychus (Acts 20). Many believers were raised at the time of Jesus' death (Matthew 27). The most significant resurrection, of course, was Jesus himself (Matthew 28). Jesus' resurrection presented his decisive triumph over the power of sin and death.

"Crucifixion" by Andrea del Castagno

Jesus' Crucifixion

Jesus' crucifixion followed typical Roman procedures. He was publicly whipped, forced to carry his own cross, and nailed to it. A tablet identifying him was attached to the upright above his head. Contrary to custom, however, his legs were not broken to hasten his death, since he was already dead when the soldiers came to do it. The Book of John states (19:36) that this fulfilled an Old Testament prophecy.

The Acts of the Apostles: After the Resurrection

The Book of Acts tells the story of the early Christian church, written by Luke as a sequel to his account of Jesus. Luke showed the movement of the newly proclaimed message of Jesus Christ from its Jerusalem-based beginnings rooted in Judaism to its becoming a world-wide, inclusive faith that reached all the way to Rome.

Messiah: One Who is Anointed

Our word *Messiah* comes from the Hebrew word *mashiach*, which means "anointed one." In the Old Testament, kings were anointed into their office; so any number of kings could be called messiahs. The New Testament presents Jesus as the Messiah, the one ultimate and perfect king.

"Abba, Father"

The Aramaic word *abba* is an intimate form of the word *ab*, which means "father." It was an informal term of intimacy and respect used by children, something like da-da or daddy. Jesus used this term in Mark 14:36 to describe the intimacy that believers could have with God the Father.

"Savior of the World" by Andrea del Sarto

45

The Annunciation

Jesus: One Who Saves

The name Jesus (in Greek *Iesous*) is related to the Hebrew names Joshua and Isaiah, which mean "one who saves" or "Yahweh saves." The angel told Jesus' mother, Mary, to call him Jesus, because he would save his people from their sins (Matthew 1:21).

Immanuel: God With Us

One of the most famous prophecies about the Messiah is found in Isaiah 7:14, where a virgin is to conceive and bear a son named Immanuel. This name is *Imma-nu-el* in Hebrew, literally translated it means "with us (is) God." Matthew 1:23 quotes this as having been fulfilled in Jesus.

Jesus, the Christ

Christ was not part of the name that Mary gave Jesus. The term is a title, and it comes from the Greek word for "messiah" (*christos*). Thus, Jesus was often referred to as "the Christ" (the Messiah). Jesus' friends would have called him *Yeshua*, the Aramaic word for Jesus.

"Christ and the Pharisees" by Jakob Jordaens

Romans: Paul's System of Faith

The Book of Romans is a letter written to Christians in Rome to explain Paul's understanding of what the Christian faith was about. This book is the most systematic and theological of his letters. The first half emphasizes the theme of righteousness and how to attain it, and the last chapters are practical exhortations about living.

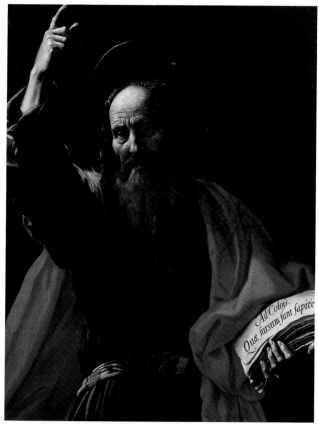

"Saint Paul" by Rutilio Manetti

INRI: Jesus of Nazareth, King of the Jews

All four Gospels state that a plaque was placed on Jesus' cross identifying him. John states that it was written in Hebrew, Latin, and Greek. The letters "INRI," often seen on this plaque in paintings of Jesus' crucifixion, represent the Latin words for the phrase, "Jesus of Nazareth, King of the Jews."

A Secret Password

The fish was an early symbol of Christianity, since the Greek word for fish, *ichthus*, is an acronym (the first letter of each word) for the Greek phrase *Iesous Christos Theou Huios Soter*, which means "Jesus Christ, of God the Son, Savior." It was written as graffiti, and was used as a secret password when Christians were being persecuted by the Romans.

Temple of Apollo at Corinth

1 and 2 Corinthians: Problem Solving

The church at Corinth, Greece, had many problems. Paul's letters to them—there were at least four, but only two are preserved—address these problems one by one. These problems included factions in the church, incest, marriage, food offered to idols, spiritual gifts (such as speaking in unintelligible tongues), opposition to Paul, and the concept of resurrection.

Galatians: Freedom from Legalism

Since all the early Christians were Jews, a question arose about Christians keeping all the Jewish laws, including circumcision. This letter was Paul's statement that Christians were made right with God only by their faith.

Psalms, Hymns, and Spiritual Songs

The Apostle Paul twice mentions the songs of Christian worship in his letters. He urges people to sing "psalms and hymns and spiritual songs" with great joy and thanksgiving (Ephesians 5:19; Colossians 3:16). These included the words of Scripture (psalms), as well as songs of praise (hymns) and other types of songs (spiritual songs).

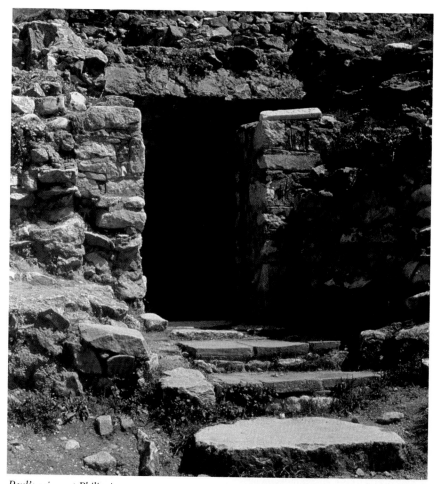

Paul's prison at Philippi

Ephesians, Philippians, Colossians: Prison Letters

The Apostle Paul spent much time in prison for his faith, and there he wrote several letters to churches. In these letters, he encouraged three different churches to know clearly what they believe and to put these beliefs into practice.

An Early Christian Hymn

The Apostle Paul occasionally used the words of early Christian hymns in writing his letters. The most famous example is in Philippians 2:5–11, where a soaring passage about Christ's humility, humiliation, and ultimate exaltation is found.

1 and 2 Thessalonians: The End of Time

Paul gave the church at Thessalonica, Greece, encouragement and instruction in these two letters. This included much teaching about the return of Christ to earth at the end of time. This church must have had a special interest in the subject.

Thessalonica

1 and 2 Timothy, Titus: Pastoral Letters

These letters were to two people who were ministers (or pastors) of churches. The letters gave specific instructions about the orderly functioning of churches, and for resisting false teachings.

Inter-Biblical Quotes

The New Testament quotes the Old Testament hundreds of times, but only once does a New Testament author mention another New Testament writer by name. Peter cites Paul in support of his own views on God's patience (2 Peter 3:15).

"Saint Paul in Prison" by Rembrandt

Philemon: On Slavery

This is one of Paul's most intensely personal letters. It is a friendly, tactful letter to his friend Philemon, who owned a runaway slave. This slave had been captured, and he converted to Christianity under Paul in prison. Paul asked Philemon to welcome the slave as he would welcome Paul.

"Jesus Comforts the Women of Jerusalem" by Martin Feuerstein

Hebrews: Book of Better Things

The author of this book forcefully makes the point that Jesus was the perfect fulfillment of much prophecy in the Old Testament. The book stresses the importance of faith.

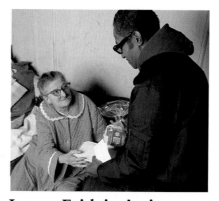

James: Faith in Action

Whereas Romans, Galatians, and Hebrews stress the importance of faith alone in one's relationship to God, the Book of James presents the case that faith without good works to demonstrate this faith is dead intellectualism.

Fables in the Bible

Fables are fictitious stories that make a concise moral point; they often employ animals or plants as speaking characters. A well-known fable in the Bible is the one told by Jotham about the trees. It begins "The trees once went forth to anoint a king over them; and they said to the olive tree, 'Reign over us.'"

Olive branches

Jericho Road

"Herod" by James J. Tissot

Herod the Fox

Metaphors are figures of speech in which a term describing a certain object is used to describe something else for the purpose of making a vivid comparison. This was a rhetorical device that Jesus often used. He called King Herod "that fox" (Luke 13:32). He called himself "the bread of life" (John 6:35) and "the true vine" (John 15:1). He even called some who came to follow him "you brood of vipers!" (Luke 3:7).

Hagar the Mountain

An allegory is a story that carries (or gives in its interpretation) a hidden meaning, or, more commonly, several hidden meanings. A well-known example is from the Apostle Paul, when he speaks of Abraham's two wives, Sarah and Hagar. He says "Now this is an allegory: these women are two covenants.... Now Hagar is Mount Sinai...." (Galatians 4:24,25). He also compares Hagar with the earthly Jerusalem and Sarah with the heavenly city.

Fanciful Interpretation

Allegorical interpretation was popular early in church history. Here is part of one early church father's (Origen's) interpretation of the parable of the Good Samaritan:

The man going down to Jericho = Adam
Jerusalem, his starting-point = Paradise
Jericho = This world
Robbers = Hostile influences and enemies
Wounds = Sins
Priest = Law
Levites = Prophets
Good Samaritan = Christ
Beast = Body of Christ
Inn = Church
Innkeeper = Guardian angels
Return of Good Samaritan = Second coming of Christ

"Hagar and Ishmael in the Desert" by Claude le Lorrain

1 and 2 Peter: Crisis Management

The Apostle Peter's two letters offer encouragement to those suffering persecution. Peter reminds them of their fellow sufferer and the perfect example, Jesus. These letters also warn against false teachings.

1, 2, and 3 John: Truth and Love

John's letters deal with truth in the face of false teaching, especially early Gnosticism (intellectual knowledge can lead to salvation). In his first letter, he also emphasizes right relationship with God through Jesus Christ, and the importance of love in all areas of our life.

Jude: Eclectic Warnings

This short book warns against false teachings, much in the way that 2 Peter does. A distinctive aspect of Jude is that it quotes from non-biblical books, such as the Assumption of Moses (in verse 9) and the Book of Enoch (in verse 14).

Saint John writes his book.

"Apocalypse of St. John" tapestry

Revelation: Visions of the End

The Book of Revelation presents the Apostle John's visions of the end of time. The book is rich with symbols and strange creatures, such as angels, dragons, and beasts, great armies and cataclysmic battles, a lake of fire, and a bottomless pit. The consistent message of the book is the ultimate and final triumph of Christ over the devil and all forces of evil.

"Saint Jerome in His Studio" by Antonello da Messina

A Bold Translator

Latin was the language of the Roman Empire, and so, in about A.D. 382, Pope Damasus I commissioned Jerome to produce an authoritative translation of the Bible. Jerome did, but he shocked the world by translating directly from the Hebrew text, rather than from the Greek Septuagint or earlier Latin versions, as had been the practice. His version was called the Vulgate.

One of the four horsemen of the Apocalypse

Beasts and Dragons

The Book of Revelation is the longest example of apocalyptic literature in the Bible. It speaks of great hosts of angels, and a great red dragon with seven heads and ten horns and seven crowns on its heads. It describes several beasts, one that looked like a leopard with feet like a bear's and a mouth like a lion's. The dragon and the beasts are symbols of the devil.

Gutenberg's Bible: The World's First Printed Book

A German named Johann Gutenberg produced the first printed Bible in 1456. It was written in Latin, the language of the Catholic Church. Gutenberg experimented for many years in developing his printing press before he perfected what people called artificial writing. There are fewer than 50 copies of the Gutenberg Bible in existence today.

The Printing Press: A Revolutionary Technology

When the Bible was copied by hand, copies were too expensive for common people. Also, copy mistakes crept into the process. The invention of the printing press revolutionized production of the Bible and other books. Now hundreds—and even thousands—of copies could be printed, each exactly the same as the other. This made it possible for almost anyone to have a Bible.

Bible Printing Today

Modern Bibles are printed using space-age technologies. The pages still must be pressed onto blank sheets of paper, but this is now done by lightning-fast methods. There are better ways of transferring the ink onto paper, better inks, and better paper. Also, the Bible is now on computer disk and on audiocassette tapes in many languages. Many Bibles are red-letter editions, where Jesus' words are printed in red ink.

WYCLIFFE

Gutenberg's Printing Press

Each page of Gutenberg's Bible was produced by using hundreds of pieces of *movable type* made from molten lead, tin, and other metals. Each piece represented a letter. These made up the printing plates, which were held in a bed, and the ink was rolled over them. Then an impression of each page was literally pressed onto blank sheets of paper, which were held by a platen. The type used in Gutenberg's Bible looks very much like handwriting.

The First English Bibles

The first complete English Bible was not the King James Bible. It was John Wycliffe's translation in the late 1300s, based on the Latin Vulgate. It was the main English version until William Tyndale's version appeared, about 1525. Tyndale translated the Old Testament directly from the Hebrew, the first version since Jerome's to do so.

Geneva, Switzerland

The Geneva Bible

An English Bible was produced in 1560 at Geneva, Switzerland, the city of John Calvin. It was the first to print each verse as a separate paragraph, and it introduced the convention (which remains even today in the King James Bible) of italicizing words that were not in the original languages but were added by the translators in order to make sense of a passage.

"James I of England"

The King James Bible

King James I of England commissioned a unique Bible, without doctrinal marginal notes (which were common in other Bibles of the time). It was written in the common English language of the day, and it appeared in 1611. This Bible achieved a remarkable success, maintaining its place as the preeminent English Bible for well over 300 years.

The World's Oldest Bible Publisher

The longest-running publisher of Bibles is the Cambridge University Press. The Press began in 1591 with the Geneva Version of the Bible, and it has continued ever since. Today it still has a reputation of producing fine-quality Bibles.

William Tyndale's Bible: Inflammatory Version

When Tyndale was working on his English translation, Church officials were the Bible authorities. His translation threatened the Church's monopoly on Bible learning, so he had to have his English Bible printed in Germany. Because of this, Tyndale was arrested and burned to death at the stake. Thousands of copies of his Bible were seized and publicly burned.

So Many Bible Versions!

Major revisions of the King James Bible began in 1885, and have continued to the present. There has been a virtual explosion of Bible translations in the past three decades. The English-speaking public has more than 70 versions of the Bible (or parts of it) to choose from!

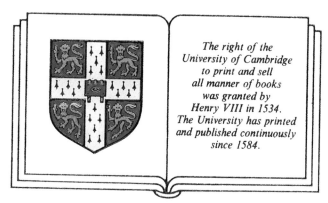

The right of the University of Cambridge to print and sell all manner of books was granted by Henry VIII in 1534. The University has printed and published continuously since 1584.

☙⊱ ABOUT THE BIBLE ⊰☙

The Wicked Bible

Some humorous typographical errors were made in early editions of the King James Bible. Probably the most famous was the omission of the word "not" in the seventh commandment, and thus it read "Thou shalt commit adultery." This edition was dubbed the Wicked Bible. For this error, the King's printers were fined 300 pounds by the archbishop!

Paraphrase Versions

Some English versions are not, strictly speaking, translations, but rather paraphrases. Translators have rewritten and paraphrased entire sentences or verses, often making two or three sentences out of a short phrase or sentence in other versions. The Living Bible and Today's English Version (Good News for Modern Man) are the most famous paraphrases. These are especially helpful for first-time Bible readers.

Literal Bible Versions

Many English Bible versions aim at word-for-word accuracy—at literal translation. That is the principle that has guided such versions as the King James Bible and its revisions, which include the New American Standard Version, the Revised Standard Version, and the New King James Version. These Bibles are useful for careful study.

"Monk Reading" by Eduard Grutzner

Dynamic Bible Versions

Most modern English Bible versions aim at "dynamic equivalency"—which means they are translated phrase-by-phrase, or thought-by-thought. These versions aren't translated strictly word-for-word. These are smoother translations and are good for reading large portions of Scripture. These include the New International Version, the Revised English and American Bibles, and the Jewish Publication Society's *Tanakh*.

Abridged Bibles

A number of condensed Bibles have appeared in the twentieth century, where repetitive portions were deleted and other portions were briefly summarized. The Reader's Digest Bible is a true abridgement. It retains the text of the Revised Standard Version, but repetitive sections, unnecessary words, and portions thought to be less important than others have been deleted. It is a good Bible for people who have never read the Bible before.

Children's Bibles

Many Bibles written especially for children also exist. Some are mostly pictures and simple retellings of Bible stories. These are simple enough for two-to-three-years-olds to understand. Others are written for grade-school children who have beginning reading vocabularies. Many have questions after each story. Other editions are written for teenagers. There are even comic book editions of the Bible!

A Down-Home Bible

Clarence Jordan's Cottonpatch Version of the Bible used contemporary Southern people, places, and parties in place of the biblical ones. Corinth became Atlanta, Jews became whites and Gentiles became Negroes, and Rome became Washington, D.C.

Rome, Italy

Best-selling Book

The Bible is consistently the world's best-selling book. Between 1815 and 1975, an estimated 2.5 billion Bibles were printed. The best-selling versions are the King James Version, the New International Version, and the Living Bible, which sell millions each year. In addition, millions of copies of the Bible and portions of it are given away free each year.

A Seaman's Bible

Paraphrasing with a vengeance was Captain J. Rogers' practice in his Seaman's Version of the Bible. In Psalm 23, for example, instead of the familiar "The Lord is my shepherd, I shall not want," Rogers had "The Lord is my Pilot; I shall not drift."

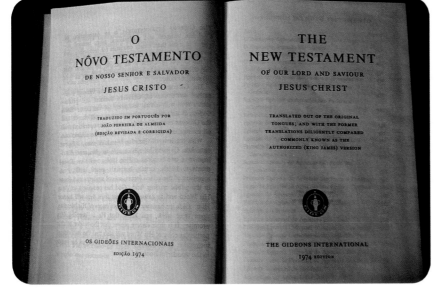

Bible Translations

Portions of the Bible have been translated into about 2,000 of the more than 6,000 known languages today, including close to 400 complete Bible translations. Most of the world's languages are minor languages of small, remote tribes or groups. Many organizations work at translating the Bible into most of the remaining languages. The goal is not 100 percent though, since many people can speak or read more than their own native language.

Unrolled amulet

The Earliest Biblical Texts

The earliest biblical texts in existence today are two short fragments found inscribed on two beautiful silver amulets. These were discovered in 1979 alongside the Scottish Church in Jerusalem. They date to about the time of the destruction of Jerusalem in 587 B.C., and they contain the words of Numbers 6:22–27. This is the priestly benediction known as the Aaronic Blessing.

The Most Expensive Bible

The world's most expensive Bible is the copy of Gutenberg's Old Testament, containing Genesis through Psalms. It was printed in 1455, and it brought $5.39 million at an auction at Christie's in New York on October 22, 1987.

The Oldest Hebrew Bible

The oldest complete version of the Hebrew Bible still in existence dates from A.D. 1008. It is part of a valuable and comprehensive collection of old Hebrew manuscripts in the Russian Public Library in St. Petersburg (formerly Leningrad), brought there in the late 1800s. It is known as the Leningrad Codex.

Codex Sinaiticus

The Oldest Greek New Testament

The oldest complete version of the New Testament (as well as the Greek Old Testament) is a book written on parchment dating to the fourth century A.D. It is called the Codex Sinaiticus, because it was discovered in a monastery on Mount Sinai in the middle of the 1800s. It was purchased from the Soviet government in 1933 by the British government for 100,000 pounds, and it is now in the British Museum in London.

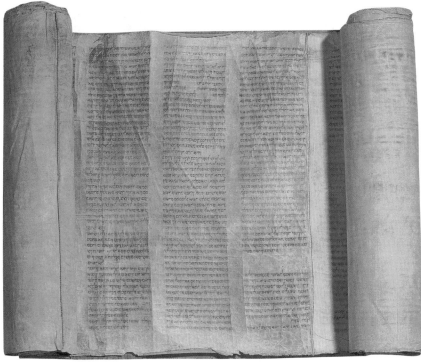

Fifteenth century Hebrew Pentateuch

The Samaritan Pentateuch

An early Hebrew version was the popularizing revision of the Bible's first five books (the Pentateuch) made in the Samaritan community north of Jerusalem, which arose some time after 722 B.C. It differs in some 6,000 places with the major Hebrew manuscripts available today. Many are trivial differences, but some reflect the Samaritans' emphasis on certain of their own doctrines.

Where's That Reference Again?

The Bible was not written with chapter or verse numbers, which made it difficult to locate specific texts. The first paragraph markings of the Hebrew Bible were before the Christian Era, and division by verse was introduced by Jewish scribes soon after the time of Christ. Chapter divisions of both Old and New Testaments came in the thirteenth century.

Can't They Count?!

In many places, the verse numbering in the English Old Testament differs slightly from that in the Hebrew Bible, even though the contents are exactly the same. Most often this happens in Psalms, where English Bibles do not number the titles of the ancient psalms, while the Hebrew Bible does.

Samaritan Distinctives

The Samaritans were Israelites who arose in and around Samaria and Mount Gerizim after the Assyrians sacked the city in 722 B.C. They were conservative in doctrine: They only accepted the Pentateuch as Scripture. Occasionally they made changes for doctrinal reasons, such as the substitution of Mount Gerizim (which was their sacred mountain) for Mount Ebal in Deuteronomy 27:4, as the place where the law was to be written on the altar.

Mount Gerizim

The Talmud: Jewish Teaching

The Hebrew word *talmud* means both "learning" and "teaching." As a title, it refers to two great collections of Jewish learning, which are based upon the Bible. These are the exhaustive Babylonian Talmud, collected in the fifth century A.D. and the shorter Jerusalem Talmud, collected somewhat earlier. The Pharisees were the guardians of the Jewish traditions that made their way into the Talmud.

What is the Tanakh?

This is what Jews call their Bible, and it is the acronym for the Hebrew Bible. The word is based upon the three divisions of the Hebrew Bible: the Law, the Prophets, and the Writings. The Hebrew words for these are *Torah*, *Nebi'im*, and *Kethubim*. The first letters of these three words are T-N-K, which come together in the word Tanakh.

The Mishnah: Collection of Jewish Law and Ethics

The Mishnah ("teaching by repetition") is the first part (and core) of the Talmud and ranks second only to the Bible itself. It is divided into six parts. The first is Seeds, which are eleven tractates dealing with agricultural regulations. The second is Festivals, which are twelve tractates (treatises) dealing with the festivals. The third is Women, which are seven tractates on marriage and divorce. The fourth is Damages—these are ten tractates on civil and criminal laws. The fifth is Sacred Things, which are eleven tractates on sacrifices. The last and sixth is Cleanness—these twelve tractates are on ritual cleanness and uncleanness.

The Gemara: Amplification of the Mishnah

The Gemara ("learning") is the second part of the Talmud, and it amplifies and comments upon the Mishnah, the Talmud's first part. It was written in Aramaic (the Mishnah was written in Hebrew). Together, the Mishnah and the Gemara comprise the full Talmud. The Babylonian Talmud is 5,894 folio pages in length, and is 12 large volumes.

"The ocean of the Talmud"

The subject matter of the Babylonian Talmud (which has been the standard Talmud for most Jews) is so extensive that the phrase "the ocean of the Talmud" arose to describe it. A prominent editor of the *Encyclopedia of Jewish Concepts* comments that it includes "religion and ethics, exegesis and homiletics, jurisprudence and ceremonial laws, ritual and liturgy, philosophy and science, medicine and magic, astronomy and astrology, history and geography, commerce and trade, politics and social problems."

✤ ABOUT THE BIBLE ✤

The Wisdom of the Talmud

Many sayings in the Talmud are reminiscent of those in the Book of Proverbs. Here are some samples: "I have learned much from my teachers, even more from my colleagues, but I have learned the most from my students." "He who seeks a friend without faults will remain friendless." "No one should taunt a reformed sinner about his past."

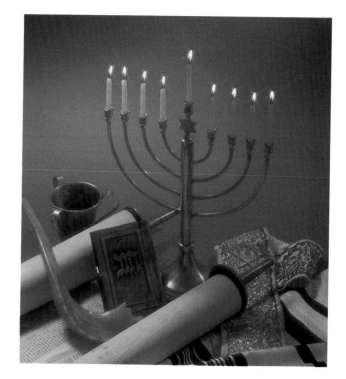

Midrash: Jewish Commentary

The term *midrash* means "investigation" or "commentary." Many books called midrashes arose between A.D. 200 and 1000, commenting on books of the Hebrew Bible from legal, ethical, or devotional perspectives. The midrashes contain many stories with morals to them (like Aesop's fables) and many ethical maxims.

A Rabbi's Good Advice

Constant study of the Law was very important in the Jewish community. Psalm 1:2 states that the righteous person's delight is in meditating day and night on the Law. The great rabbi Hillel encouraged frequent repetition in such study by saying that "reviewing a lesson a hundred times cannot be compared with reviewing it a hundred and one times."

A Man and His Wife in the Talmud

The Talmud contains many wise sayings about marriage: "Love your wife as much as yourself, but honor her more than yourself." "If your wife is short, bend your head and take her advice." "A man should eat and drink beneath his means, clothe himself within his means, and honor his wife above his means."

The Masoretes: Jewish Guardians of the Scriptures

Hebrew was originally written without vowels, spaces between words, or punctuation. The Masoretes were Jewish scribes who first appeared in the second century A.D. and who flourished in the sixth through tenth centuries A.D. They devised a system of word, phrase, sentence, and paragraph divisions, as well as a detailed system for representing the vowels and accents on words. This insured that the Hebrew Scriptures would be uniformly copied, pronounced, and interpreted.

Hebrew scroll from Qumran

The Masorah: A Fence for the Law

The system of vowel and accent markings, as well as the Masoretes' many marginal notations about individual words and phrases, was called the Masorah. It protected the biblical text from misunderstanding and misinterpretation. A famous rabbinic quote about the Masorah is that it serves as "a fence for the Torah," i.e., to protect it.

The Torah: The Ladder of Sinai

Jacob dreamed about a ladder he saw ascending into heaven. The numerical value of the Hebrew word for ladder equals that of the word Sinai. Thus, the rabbis argued that the Torah—the Law of Moses—which was revealed at Mount Sinai, was the ladder that leads from earth to heaven.

"The Vision of Jacob's Ladder" by Raphael

66

Jeremiah prophesies to the people.

The Longest Book in the Bible

The Book of Jeremiah is the longest book in the Bible. It has the most words, even though it doesn't have the most chapters (52). Jeremiah was a passionate prophet, pouring out his heart at great length and with great emotion to God. The book with the most chapters is the Book of Psalms, with 150 separate psalms.

The Longest Verse in the Bible

The Book of Esther contains the longest verse in the Bible: Esther 8:9. It consists of 85 words in the New Revised Standard Version, 43 words in the Hebrew. Its subject matter is rather mundane: It tells of Mordechai (Esther's uncle) issuing an edict.

The Longest Chapter in the Bible

The longest chapter in the Bible is Psalm 119, with 176 verses. It is an acrostic poem, with each group of eight verses beginning with successive letters of the alphabet. This psalm is a massive composition in praise of the Torah (the Law). Each verse refers to God's Word in some way.

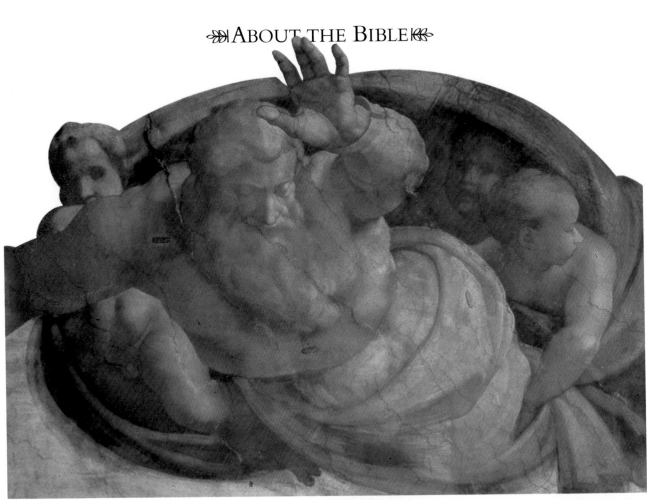

"God Dividing the Waters and the Earth" by Michelangelo

The Shortest Chapter in the Bible

The Bible's shortest chapter comes just two chapters before its longest chapter: Psalm 117. It is a beautiful little gem, a burst of praise to God, urging people to praise God for his goodness and faithfulness. It is only two verses long!

The Shortest Verse in the Bible

The Bible's shortest verse is John 11:35, "Jesus wept." This happened when Jesus heard that his friend Lazarus had died, so he performed a miracle and brought Lazarus back from the dead.

Tomb of Lazarus in Bethany

The Shortest Book in the Bible

The Book of 3 John is the shortest book in the Bible, with 19 less words than its companion book, 2 John. Both of these were about one papyrus sheet in length. Five books share the distinction of being only one chapter long: Obadiah (in the Old Testament) and Philemon, 2 John, 3 John, and Jude (in the New Testament).

The Most Wives

Solomon had the most recorded wives in the Bible: 300 wives who were princesses and 700 concubines (female slaves). Many of his marriages were political. They were tokens of an alliance with a foreign king with whom Solomon had exchanged daughters in exchange for promises of peace.

"Solomon and His Harem" by James J. Tissot

"Noah's Ark" by Sir Edwin Landseer

Methuselah: Just One of the Boys

Many people know that Methuselah was the oldest man in the Bible, living 969 years. However, he was not unique for his time. Jared lived for 962 years, Noah lived for 950 years, Seth lived for 912 years, Enosh lived for 905 years, and Mahalalel lived for 895 years. The first man, Adam, lived for 930 years.

The Tallest Man in the Bible

Goliath was the Bible's tallest man. He was a Philistine giant who measured "six cubits and a span," or about 9½ feet tall. King Saul was also tall. His height is given as being "head and shoulders above everyone else."

Zacchaeus views Jesus from a tree.

The Shortest Man in the Bible

No short person's height is actually given, but Zacchaeus was noted for his short stature. Luke 19 tells us that when Jesus came to town, Zacchaeus climbed a tree to see him because he (Zacchaeus) was too short to see over the crowd. Some people joke that Job's friend Bildad the Shuhite ("shoe-height") was the world's shortest man.

"David's Victory Over Goliath" by Caravaggio

The Most Husbands

The Sadducees told Jesus of a woman who had had seven husbands, all brothers (Matthew 22). Each one had died, and the next had married the woman. Jesus himself encountered a woman who had had five husbands, and who was currently living with a man who was not her husband (John 4).

The Smallest Seed

The smallest seed mentioned in the Bible is the tiny mustard seed. The mustard plant grew into something close to five feet tall, however. Jesus used it to characterize the growth of God's kingdom, from something small (the tiny seed) to something great (the large plant), as well as to speak of the tiny amount of faith needed to work wonders.

Mustard plants

The Most Generous Person in the Bible

This honor belongs to the poor widow Jesus saw dropping two small copper coins into the treasury boxes in the Temple. These were the smallest coins in circulation, worth less than a penny, and yet they were the last things she owned. Thus, she gave "all she had to live on" (Mark 12:44).

Twenty-Four Fingers and Toes!

A Philistine giant mentioned in 1 Chronicles 20:6 had six fingers on each hand and six toes on each foot. This phenomenon (called polydactylism) is commonly known from ancient texts and art. In an early temple in Jericho, a six-toed clay statue was found. In Assyria, a child with six fingers on the left hand was considered a good sign, but six fingers on the right hand was a sign of bad fortune.

"The Widow's Mite" by A. D. Rahn

Language and Literature

A is for Ox

The earliest alphabets used pictures of common objects to represent the sounds of the first letters of these words. The first letter of the Hebrew alphabet is the *aleph*, derived from *alpu* "ox," and so the first *aleph* was a line drawing of an ox head. Through a series of linguistic steps, it is the ancestor of the English capital *A*.

An Alphabet Story

A rabbinic story tells how each letter asked God to create the world using a word that began with it. However, beginning from the end of the alphabet, each letter was disqualified, because an unfavorable word also began with it. This lasted until the second letter (*beth*), which was given the honor: The word *bara* ("to create") begins with *beth*. The first letter of the alphabet (*aleph*) had the honor of beginning the Ten Commandments.

"Moses Breaketh the Tablets" by Edward Lanning

Let's Learn the Aleph-Beth!

The English word alphabet traces its origins to Hebrew. It comes from the first two Greek letters, *alpha* and *beta*. But the Greeks borrowed their alphabet from the Phoenicians (close cousins to the Hebrews), whose alphabet began with *aleph* and *beth*, the Phoenician-Hebrew words for "ox" and "house."

Tittle   Jot

Jots and Tittles

When Jesus said, "one jot or one tittle shall in no way pass from the law, till all be fulfilled" (Matthew 5:18), he affirmed the importance of the Old Testament law. The "jot" was the *yodh*, the smallest letter of the Hebrew alphabet, while the "tittle" was only part of a letter: a small pen stroke.

Blessings From A to Z

In Jewish tradition, God blesses Israel from "aleph to taw." These Hebrew letters are the first and last in the Hebrew alphabet, so the expression means God blesses Israel completely. By striking coincidence, the list of blessings found in Leviticus 26:3–13 begins with aleph and ends with taw!

"Saint Augustine" by Botticelli

Lip-Reading

St. Augustine once saw St. Ambrose reading the Bible silently. This surprised him so much that he commented on the fact that Ambrose was reading "without moving his lips." In the ancient world, reading—even to oneself—was always done aloud.

"Two Monks" by Barlach

Ancient Scribes

The scribes were the ancient world's educated elite. They were the guardians of the very complex writing traditions, which required years of study to master. Scribes learned in scribal schools, where they copied ancient texts by the dozen. They served kings in all societies, including Israel and Judah.

Scribes as Religious Authorities

After Jerusalem and the Temple were destroyed by the Babylonians in 586 B.C., the study of the Mosaic Law (the Torah) grew in importance, and the scribes became a professional class of Torah scholars. In the New Testament, Jesus had many disputes over interpretation of the Law with the scribes and Pharisees.

Strange Meditations

The Hebrew word for "meditation" (*hagah*) is also used to describe the coo of a dove, the growl of a lion, the plotting of evil rulers, as well as the reading of the Bible. These things are all something done audibly. Thus, when Jews were instructed to "meditate" on God's word (Psalm 1:2), this meant that they should recite it aloud to themselves.

"Woe Unto You, Scribes and Pharisees" by James J. Tissot

75

Ashurbanipal's Library

The Assyrian king Ashurbanipal was by far the greatest patron of literature in the pre-Christian Era. He amassed a royal library of more than 26,000 historical, religious, and scientific texts at his capital of Nineveh. He commissioned his emissaries to search the world and bring back copies of every known text. The discovery of this library in 1853 revealed a large portion of what we know today of ancient Mesopotamia.

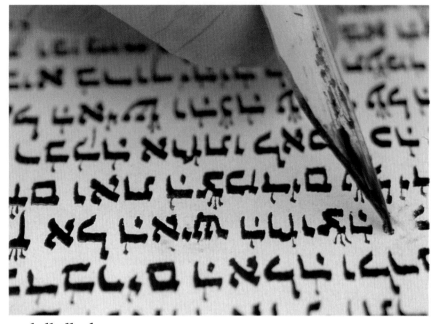

mrhdlttllmb

This is "Mary had a little lamb," written without any vowels, word divisions, or punctuation. The Old Testament was originally written without any of these, and readers had to supply these themselves in order to make sense of the text.

Ancient Law Codes

The Mosaic Law contains 613 specific commandments regulating most aspects of people's lives and worship, but this is not the earliest example of an ancient law code. The Sumerians developed the first such codes in the early second millennium B.C. The most systematic law code was the Babylonian king Hammurabi's (about 1792 to 1750 B.C.), and the Hittites also developed an extensive law code in the thirteenth century B.C.

Scapegoat or Demon?

The word "scapegoat" comes from the King James Version of the Bible. In Leviticus 16, a goat was banished to the wilderness after Israel's sins were symbolically transferred onto its head (the "escape goat"). However, the Hebrew term in question, *azazel*, was probably the name of a desert demon, and the goat was sent "to Azazel" (to remove Israel's sin completely).

❧ LANGUAGE AND LITERATURE ❧

Did Adam Speak Hebrew?

The words of Adam recorded in the Scriptures are in Hebrew, but he probably did not speak this language. Hebrew was not identifiable as a language until the second half of the second millennium B.C. Therefore, we do not know the precise language of early Bible people such as Adam, Noah, or Abraham.

"Sermon on the Mount" by Hendrick Krock

The Language of Jesus

Aramaic, which is closely related to Hebrew, was the language that Jesus spoke. It all but died out in the centuries following Jesus' day. Amazingly, the language still survives today, but only in isolated villages in Syria, Turkey, Iraq, and Iran. Assyrian Christians from northern Iraq still speak it today as well.

Adam

A Roll of the Dice

The festival of Purim got its name from a rare word meaning "lot" (Hebrew *pur*). This festival celebrates the reversal of events that had been determined by Haman, the Jews' enemy, by casting lots or dice. An example of such a die, from Assyria, was found recently, dating to the ninth century B.C. It is a small, six-sided clay cube with the word *pur* on it.

Coming or Going?

An early way of writing among the Greeks—soon abandoned—was done in a forward-backward mode, like a field is plowed. The Greek term for this was *boustrophedon* (which means "as the ox turns"). Here is a familiar nursery rhyme written this way:

Humpty Dumpty sat on a wall
ytpmuD ytpmuH
had a great fall.
sesroh s'gnik eht llA
and all the king's men
ytpmuH tup t'ndluoc
together again.

77

Abracadabra

This word was probably an Aramaic magical word. It was used to ward off fever or inflammation, and, in the Middle Ages, patients were advised to wear it on an amulet to ward off and cure diseases. The word was probably written in this manner:

A B R A C A D A B R A
A B R A C A D A B R
A B R A C A D A B
A B R A C A D A
A B R A C A D
A B R A C A
A B R A C
A B R A
A B R
A B
A

Dentists in the Bible?

The prophet Amos, like most of the prophets, often used picturesque language to make his point. In one passage, to illustrate that God had used famine to try to jolt Israel out of its spiritual lethargy, he says that God gave Israel "cleanness of teeth" (Amos 4:6). This is not a reference to personal hygiene, but instead means they had no food to get between their teeth.

You Devil, You!

The word "devil" comes from Greek *diabolos* ("slanderer"), while "Satan" comes from Hebrew *satan* ("adversary"). The New Testament gives us most of our information about the devil, showing him as a malevolent reality, always opposed to God and his people, and whose power will be crushed in the end. He appears in many forms, such as a serpent, a dragon, a sea monster, a flash of lightning, an angel of light, and a roaring lion.

Beelzebub: Lord of the Flies

In William Golding's novel, the lord of the flies was a pig's head worshiped by choirboys-turned-savages. In the Old Testament, Beelzebub was the name of an important Philistine god. In the New Testament, Jesus was accused of driving out demons by the power of Beelzebul (the New Testament word is spelled differently), a reference to Satan, the prince of demons.

❧ LANGUAGE AND LITERATURE ❧

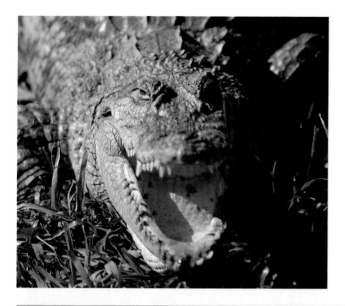

The Loch Ness Monster, Too?

Leviathan is a Hebrew name referring to some type of large water creature. In Psalm 104:26, it is clearly a sea creature, possibly a whale or a dolphin. In Job 41:1–34, however, an extended description makes it sound like a crocodile. The Hebrew term was probably deliberately vague, to accommodate all sorts of water monsters.

Hippopotami and Football Players

The Hebrew word *behemoth* is a rare word for "beasts." In Job 40:15, it refers to a large animal, probably the hippopotamus. Many English versions merely render it as behemoth, however. The modern-day meaning of something large (football players as behemoths) takes its meaning from this passage.

Baal: A God or a Husband?

The Canaanite god Baal is well known in the Bible and in other literature. His name is a generic Semitic word (*baal*) meaning "lord," "master," or "owner." A specialized use of *baal* is "husband," reflecting the idea of husbands as lords over their wives.

"Mona Lisa" by Leonardo da Vinci

The Apple of Your Eye

This phrase is found five times in the King James Version of the Bible, including the prayer "Keep me as the apple of your eye." In reality, the Hebrew word here means "pupil (of the eye)," and the idea is one of God's keeping close watch over his people. Hebrew has a separate word for the fruit.

What is Anti-Semitic?

The term anti-Semitic today generally means anti-Jewish. The term "Semite" comes from Noah's oldest son Shem, however, and it refers to people who are ethnically (race) or linguistically (language) related to each other. This means that both Jews and Arabs are Semites. It is incorrect then to speak of Arabs as being anti-Semitic.

Christ enters Jerusalem on a donkey.

Ancient Words of Worship

Many Hebrew or Aramaic words are used in modern-day worship. *Hallelujah* means "Praise the Lord!" *Hosanna* was a shout of acclamation used to welcome Jesus into Jerusalem, which originally meant "Save us!" *Amen* is Hebrew for "Surely! So be it!" *Maranatha* was an Aramaic word used by Paul meaning "Our Lord, come!" (referring to hopes of Christ's return to earth).

Creation

The famous poem that begins "Only God can make a tree" obviously wasn't written by an Israelite. The Hebrew language has a special word, *bara*, that refers to God's creative acts. In Hebrew, humans can form, make, and build, and so can God, but only God can create. Since the materials out of which God creates are never mentioned with the word *bara*, we know that God creates out of nothing.

Joseph's coat

Joseph and His Amazing Technicolor Dream Coat

While this makes a good title for a Broadway musical, and the story of Jacob giving his favorite son a multicolored coat paints a gripping picture, the reference to the coat's color is not necessarily accurate. Most recent Bible versions render the phrase as "a richly ornamented robe," "an ornamented tunic," or "a long robe with sleeves."

Eve is created from Adam.

The Tale of the Tel

The Hebrew word *tel* refers to a layered mound that has been built up over the centuries by successive occupations. Most large cities in Palestine were rebuilt on the same locations, and the remains of their mounds can still be seen today. The King James Bible's translators had never seen a tel, and thus they mistranslated Joshua 11:13, which refers to "cities that stood on their mounds (tels)" as "cities that stood still in their strength."

Near Eastern Tel

Scrolls and Books

Most biblical books were originally written on scrolls, which were sheets of papyrus or parchment sewn or glued together end to end. These were somewhat unwieldy, so books were invented in the early Christian Era. The long scrolls were cut into shorter sheets, and then these were sewn together. The first books (or codexes) were inconveniently sewn together in the center of the page; later ones were sewn along the edges.

Parchment: Better "Paper"

Parchment is made mainly from the skins of sheep and goats. These skins are soaked in a lime solution, and then the hair and fat are removed by scraping and washing. The skin is stretched on a frame, dried, and then scraped smooth with pumice. Almost all copies of the Bible after the fourth century up until the invention of the printing press were written on parchment, since it is stronger and longer-lasting than papyrus.

Papyrus: Earliest Paper

Papyrus was an early, inexpensive material used as a writing surface. It was made by stripping long papyrus reeds of their bark, laying them next to each other in rows, overlaying them crosswise with more reeds, and then pounding them together. After they dried, a reasonably smooth writing surface was left. Egyptians probably discovered this process. Our word "paper" comes from *papyrus*.

Scribe writing on a codex.

An Eye for the Numbers

The Masoretes, the Jewish scribes who painstakingly and meticulously copied the Hebrew Scriptures, were so precise in their copying that they counted the number of words in each book of their Bibles, and even identified the middle word! They did this so they could check themselves and be sure they had not accidentally skipped any words.

❧ LANGUAGE AND LITERATURE ❧

Aramaic inscription

Daniel

Not All the Old Testament Is in Hebrew

While most of the Old Testament was written in Hebrew, several chapters in Ezra and Daniel (and even one verse in Jeremiah) were written in Aramaic. These sections come in contexts where international affairs are concerned, and the writers felt it advantageous to write in the lingua franca of the day.

Aramaic, the Language of Diplomats

Just as English is the international language of trade and diplomacy (or the *lingua franca*) in most of the world today, so Aramaic was during the time of Israel's monarchy. The Assyrian king Sennacherib's emissaries insulted King Hezekiah's envoys during the siege of Jerusalem by issuing demands in the local language, Hebrew, in full hearing of the common people. This was despite the envoys' request that the negotiations be conducted in Aramaic, for secrecy's sake (2 Kings 18:26–35).

Greek in the Holy Land

As ancient Greece rose in power and influence toward the end of the first millennium B.C., so did its language. It was the lingua franca during the time of Jesus. The fact that the New Testament was written in Greek, even though most of its authors were native speakers of Aramaic, attests to the language's influence and vitality.

Greek inscription

The Death of Hebrew

Hebrew began to die out as a spoken language toward the end of the Old Testament period, partly as a result of the Jews' intermarriage and assimilation. Nehemiah was distressed to find Jews who had married foreign women and whose children could not even speak "the language of Judah" (Hebrew).

A Living Language

The Hebrew Bible, or Old Testament, was written over a period of 1,000 years, primarily in Hebrew. The language changed over that time and occasionally needed to be updated. One example of this is in 1 Samuel 9:9: "In times past in Israel, this is what a man said when he went to inquire of God, 'Come, let us go to the seer.' For what is today called the prophet used to be called the seer."

Cuneiform clay tablet

How to Write on Clay

A very popular writing surface in ancient times was wet clay, which was touched with the tip of a wooden stylus to make wedge-shaped (cuneiform) impressions. Thousands of such documents have been uncovered from administrative archives in ancient cities in the Near East, including Nineveh and Babylon. Through an accident of history, these tablets were baked (and thus preserved for posterity) when cities were destroyed by fire.

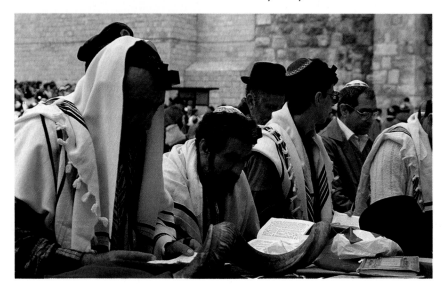

The Revival of Hebrew Today

Hebrew was kept alive only among the rabbis in the synagogues for more than 2,000 years. Then, about 100 years ago, Eliezer Ben-Yehuda, a Lithuanian Jew, proposed and worked tirelessly for its revival as a spoken language. Modern Hebrew is based upon biblical Hebrew and Talmudic Aramaic, and it has traces of Yiddish, German, and Russian.

Gezer ruins

The First Hebrew Inscription

The earliest object with a Hebrew text written on it is a limestone tablet containing a farmers' calendar. It was used in Gezer, a biblical city, almost 3,000 years ago. It reads in part:
"His two months are (olive) harvest,
His two months are planting (grain)."

The Earliest Greek Writing

A beautiful vase from eighth century B.C. Athens carries the earliest Greek inscription. It was probably a prize won in a contest, for it contains a dedication to "him who dances most delicately."

It's Carved in Stone!

The most important documents in antiquity were laboriously carved into stone, so they were permanent. The Ten Commandments were written on two stone tablets. The Babylonian king Hammurabi's Law Code was written on a hard diorite stone stele. The Moabite king Mesha's inscription about his war with Israel was inscribed on a large black basalt stone.

Balaam's Inscription

In 1967, a dramatic find was made at Tell Deir Alla in the Jordan Valley. A wall inscription dating from the eighth century B.C. mentions the biblical "Balaam son of Beor." The entire text purports to be his own inscription, telling of a night visit he had from the gods. It calls him "a seer of the gods."

Jordan River

Mesha's Stele

King Mesha's Inscription

Moabite king Mesha's inscription was carved on a large black basalt stone; it had 34 lines of text. It dates to 830 B.C., and tells of his conflicts with the Israelite kings Omri and Ahab. Mesha says of Omri, "As for Omri, king of Israel, he humbled Moab many years, for Chemosh [the Moabite god] was angry with his land."

An Egyptian Reference to Israel

The earliest reference to Israel outside of the Bible dates to about 1208 B.C., at a time when Israel had settled into the land of Canaan after following Moses out of Egypt. The Egyptian pharaoh Merneptah boasted in a victory song that he had defeated many of his enemies, including Israel: "Israel is laid waste, his seed is not."

Ostracon

Save That Broken Pot!

During Bible times, many short documents were written on *ostraca* (singular: *ostracon*), which were broken pieces of clay bowls or pots. These potsherds were just the right size on which to write a quick letter or note to someone. The writing was done with pen or brush and ink.

A Picture of an Israelite King

The only contemporary pictorial representation of an Israelite king is on the Black Obelisk of the Assyrian king Shalmaneser III. It shows Jehu, king of Israel, on his knees, presenting his tribute of valuable silver and gold items to the Assyrian king.

Giza, Egypt

The Sumerians: The First Literates

The Sumerians, the world's first literate people, lived in the same area as Abraham did years later. The Sumerians composed many texts, including great mythological epics and moving love poetry. One Sumerian text describing a victory of the city of Lagash over the city of Umma, is the world's oldest text that uses sequential sentences: It dates from the third millennium B.C.

The Rosetta Stone: Deciphering Hieroglyphics

Egyptian hieroglyphics remained a mystery until Napoleon's troops discovered a large black basalt stone at the Egyptian city of Rosetta in 1799. The stone contained an inscription written in Greek (a known language) and two types of Egyptian writing, one of which was hieroglyphics. It was deciphered by the French scholar Champollion. The stone was a decree of King Ptolemy V, who ruled over Egypt and Palestine in 204 to 180 B.C.

Rosetta Stone

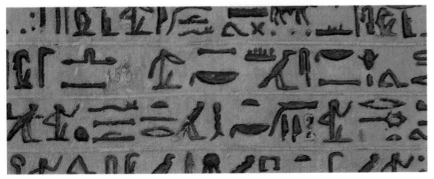

Hieroglyphics

Egyptian Hieroglyphics

When Europeans visited Egypt in the eighteenth century, they were impressed by its many wonders. One of those wonders was its mysterious writing system, which used hieroglyphs ("sacred carvings"). This system used hundreds of colorful pictures as symbols for words or sounds.

Latin manuscript

Nile River

Latin: The Language of the Roman Empire and the Church

John 19:20 states that the plaque above Jesus' head was written in "Hebrew, in Latin, and in Greek." Hebrew (or Aramaic) was the local language, Greek was the language of commerce, and Latin was the language of the Roman Empire. When the Roman Empire became Christianized in the fourth century A.D., Latin became the language of the Church. In the Roman Catholic Church, Latin remained the language for Mass until the Second Vatican Council in the 1960s.

The Lachish Letters

In 1935 and 1938, a total of 21 letters written on potsherds (ostraca) were found at biblical Lachish, a city about 30 miles southwest of Jerusalem. They are from the two to three years immediately before Jerusalem (and Lachish) fell to the Babylonians in 586 B.C. Most were letters from commanders of military outposts reporting back to the commander in Lachish. They reflect the unsettled conditions of those years.

The Elephantine Letters

In 1893, the first of several dozen letters written on papyrus and ostraca were found on a small island in the Nile River about 550 miles south of Cairo. A Jewish settlement thrived there in the fifth century B.C. These letters were primarily legal and business texts, but they show the existence of a Jewish temple and that the Jews worshiped many gods.

Assyrian relief of the siege of Lachish

Jeremiah

Assyrian relief

The Lights of Azekah

One letter found at Lachish gives a dramatic picture into the rapidly deteriorating situation in the face of the Babylonian assault. The writer informed his commander that they were now watching carefully for the fire signals from Lachish, "for we cannot see Azekah." Azekah was a town about 15 miles north of Lachish that had just fallen to the Babylonians.

The Amarna Letters

An important collection of almost 400 clay tablets was found beginning in 1887 at Tell el-Amarna on the Nile River in Middle Egypt. They date to the middle of the thirteenth century B.C. Most of these were letters from petty kings or their scribes in the land of Canaan to their Egyptian overlords. These show the period to have been one of international diplomacy, but also of constant low-level conflict.

Jeremiah: Jewish Traitor?

Jeremiah emphasized strongly that the Jews should not resist the Babylonians, since they were God's instrument to punish Judah's sins. Many in Jerusalem, however, did not like this counsel. They accused Jeremiah of being a traitor, saying that "he is weakening the hands of the soldiers who are left in this city" (Jeremiah 38:4). Strikingly, this is precisely the same phrase found in one of the Lachish letters about advice coming from Jerusalem!

Euphrates River

The Nuzi Tablets

More than 4,000 clay tablets were discovered in the 1920s at ancient Nuzi, east of the Tigris River. These date to the middle of the second millennium B.C. These texts give a wide-ranging picture of everyday life at that time, including things such as land ownership, the position of slaves and women, prices and sales of goods, occupations, legal customs, and family law. Many intriguing parallels are found in Genesis and the Nuzi documents.

The Mari Documents

An important cache of almost 20,000 clay tablets was discovered in the 1930s at ancient Mari, on the middle Euphrates River. These were found in the palace of the ancient Babylonian king Zimri-Lim, dating to around 1750 B.C. Among the documents are some 5,000 letters. These come from the land where the biblical patriarchs came from, and date to the time immediately following them.

The Babylonian Chronicles

The Babylonians, in the eighth through sixth centuries B.C., developed a unique type of historical writing called the chronicle. In several important chronicles, the events of each year are listed, along with the king at the time. These are remarkable for their straightforward reporting of the facts, and for their accurate dating, down to the exact year, month, and day.

The Fall of Babylon in a Babylonian Chronicle

The Chronicle of Nabonidus, last king of Babylon, tells of Babylon's fall to the Persian king Cyrus. It is remarkably free of the self-serving rhetoric usually found in such annals. It states that "the army of Cyrus entered Babylon without battle. Afterwards Nabonidus was arrested in Babylon when he returned there.... Cyrus entered Babylon, green twigs were spread in front of him—the state of 'Peace' was imposed upon the city. Cyrus sent greetings to all Babylon."

Jerusalem

"The Babylonian Exile" by Edward Bendemann

Cyrus' Decree in the Bible

The words of Cyrus' famous decree freeing the Jews from captivity are preserved in Ezra 1:2,3. Cyrus states "The Lord, the God of heaven, has given me all the kingdoms of the earth, and he has charged me to build him a house at Jerusalem.... Whoever is among you of all his people, may his God be with him, and let him go up to Jerusalem...and rebuild the house of the Lord, the God of Israel—he is the God who is in Jerusalem."

The Fall of Babylon in a Persian Inscription

King Cyrus of Persia captured Babylon in 539 B.C. His own account of this is much more self-serving than the Babylonian account. Cyrus states that the god Marduk "beheld with pleasure [Cyrus'] good deeds and his upright heart.... Without any battle he made him enter his town Babylon.... All the inhabitants... bowed to [Cyrus] and kissed his feet...with shining faces. Happily they greeted him as a master...and they worshiped his very name."

Persepolis of ancient Persia

✥ LANGUAGE AND LITERATURE ✥

Cyrus' Decree in His Own Words

In Cyrus' own royal inscription, he gives the god Marduk credit for ordering him to allow captive peoples to return: "I resettled upon the command of Marduk, the great lord, all the gods...unharmed, in their former chapels [temples], the places which make them happy." As a good politician, Cyrus may well have issued this as a universal decree, and then issued specific ones to each captive people in which he mentioned their specific gods.

Canaanite temple at Hazor

Ancient Receipts

Many discoveries of ancient texts from Bible lands have dazzled the public with their dramatic contents. However, by far the greatest number of ancient texts are ordinary documents of government and commerce. For example, a group of 63 ostraca were found in 1910 at Samaria, dating to the reign of Jeroboam II. They are mundane receipts, such as this one: "In the tenth year. From Hazeroth to Gaddiyahu. A jar of fine oil."

Assyrian relief

Assyrian Annals

The Assyrian kings developed the custom of mounting a yearly or every other year military campaign to conquer new lands. After each campaign, a record of it was written up. After several campaigns, several accounts of the first campaigns existed. It is interesting to note that the number of enemies killed tend to be progressively inflated in successive editions of these annals.

⚛ LANGUAGE AND LITERATURE ⚛

Bombastic Royal Rhetoric

Ancient kings loved to have themselves exalted. Here is how the account of Sennacherib's second military campaign begins: "Sennacherib, the great king, the powerful king...king of the four quarters of the world...wise shepherd, favorite of the great gods, guardian of truth, lover of justice, giver of help, who befriends the weak...a perfect man, a man of war, foremost among all kings...."

Assyrian soldier

The Fall of Jerusalem

The most traumatic event for Israel in the Old Testament was the destruction of Jerusalem in 586 B.C. by the Babylonians under Nebuchadnezzar (2 Kings 25). The city was razed, the Temple looted and destroyed, most of the people—including the king—carried away into exile, and a puppet ruler set up over the land. Even the great bronze pillars in front of the Temple were carried away.

King Sargon

Shalmaneser, Sargon, and the Fall of Samaria

The Bible tells of the Assyrian king Shalmaneser's conquest of Samaria in 722 B.C., in 2 Kings 17. However, in the Assyrian annals, King Sargon II, Shalmaneser's successor, claims the credit. The problem may be resolved by assuming that Shalmaneser was still king, but his general Sargon actually took the city.

Temple of Solomon mosaic

"The Terror of the People Being Engulfed by the Flood" by Victorio Bianchini

A Babylonian Flood Story

Many versions of an ancient flood story exist in the ancient Near East. The most famous tells of a legendary king, Gilgamesh, on a quest for eternal life. Along the way he meets Ut-napishtim, who has been given the gift of immortality by the gods. Ut-napishtim was a hero of old who had survived a flood, like Noah, by building a boat. Many details are similar to the biblical flood story.

Caveat Emptor! ("Let the Buyer Beware!")

A charming candor can be found in some of the Mari prophecies about the reliability or urgency of the prophecy. These are usually reported in a letter to the king, and several conclude with the letter's author telling the king that he may "take it or leave it." The following phrase is typical: "Let my lord do what pleases him [concerning this prophecy]." It is difficult to imagine biblical prophets saying similar things.

The Mari Prophets

The documents discovered at Mari in the 1930s contain many "prophecies" delivered by oracular speakers. These are typically messages from the gods to the king, usually with advice about going into battle or not. Compared to biblical prophecy, they are short, trivial, and contain none of the moral dimensions or demands found in the Bible.

Clay figure dancing and playing instrument

Hymn to the Moon God

Almost every ancient people produced hymns to their gods. Here is part of a Sumerian-Akkadian hymn to Sin, the moon god: "O Father...in the heavens, who is exalted?...You alone are exalted. On earth, who is exalted?... You alone are exalted.... O king of kings, exalted one, whose office no one can rival, whose divinity no god can equal.... May your beloved wife Ningal, the gracious, say to you, 'Rest, O Lord.'"

Nile River

Egyptian scribe

Hymn to the Nile

For the Egyptians, the Nile River was their lifeline, and so its gods were among the highest in the Egyptian pantheon. Here is part of a hymn to the Nile: "Hail to thee, O Nile, that issues from the earth and comes to keep Egypt alive!... The bringer of food, rich in provisions, creator of all good, lord of majesty, sweet in fragrance."

In Praise of Scribes

To be a scribe was a noble aspiration in the ancient Near East, especially in Egypt. Several compositions praise this profession. The following is a good example: "[The scribes] did not make for themselves pyramids of metal, with tombstones thereof of iron. They were not able to leave heirs in children...pronouncing their names, but they made heirs for themselves in the writings and in the books of wisdom which they composed."

Proverbs and the Wisdom of Amen-em-Opet

The close ties between Proverbs and some Egyptian wisdom can be seen in the following quotes.
Amen-em-Opet:
"Guard thyself against robbing the oppressed
And against overbearing the disabled."
"Do not associate to thyself the heated man,
Nor visit him for conversation."
Proverbs:
"Do not rob the poor, because he is poor,
or crush the afflicted at the gate" (Proverbs 22:22).
"Make no friendship with a man given to anger,
nor go with a wrathful man" (Proverbs 22:24).

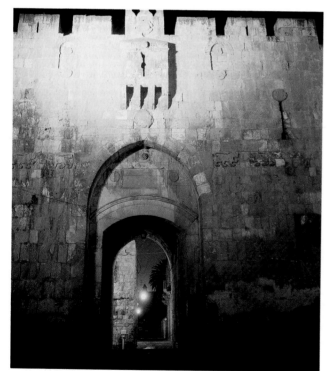

Gate in Jerusalem

The Writing of God

The Bible claims to be the word of God. However, some passages mention God's writing explicitly. The Ten Commandments were "written with the finger of God" (Exodus 31:18); they were "the writing of God" (Exodus 32:16). The pattern for the Temple is described as "the writing from the hand of the Lord" (1 Chronicles 28:19).

"God Creates the Stars and the Planets" by Michelangelo

A Strange Famine

The prophet Amos gives a startlingly vivid picture of what conditions would soon be like in Israel because of its rejection of the Lord: "I will send a famine on the land; not a famine of bread... but of hearing the words of the Lord....they shall run to and fro, to seek the word of the Lord, but they shall not find it" (Amos 8:11,12).

A Strange Meal

On two occasions, biblical characters ate a scroll that contained God's words as a symbol of internalizing them: the prophet Ezekiel (Ezekiel 2:8–3:3) and the Apostle John (Revelation 10:9,10). In both cases it tasted "sweet as honey," which echoes the words of Psalm 119:103: "How sweet are thy words to my taste, sweeter than honey to my mouth!"

Temple of Hadrian at Ephesus

Book Burning

The Bible records two occasions on which books were burned. King Jehoiakim of Judah burned the Book of Jeremiah strip by strip as it was read to him (Jeremiah 36:23). A number of magicians at Ephesus, who were converted as a result of Paul's preaching, brought their books of magic together and burned them publicly (Acts 19:19).

Malachi

Heavenly Books

In many passages, the Bible refers to books kept in heaven. Moses pleads with God to blot him out of the "book which you have written" (Exodus 32:32) for the sake of Israel's forgiveness. A psalmist asks God to "put thou my tears in thy bottle! Are they not in thy book?" (Psalm 56:8). The books of Daniel and Revelation both speak of the day that "the books were opened" (Daniel 7:10 and Revelation 20:12). Daniel refers to the "book of truth" (Daniel 10:21). The Book of Malachi speaks of a "book of remembrance" that was written about those who feared the Lord (Malachi 3:16).

And the Students Said, "Amen!"

The author of Ecclesiastes voiced the complaints of endless generations of students when he said, "Of making many books there is no end, and much study is a weariness of the flesh" (Ecclesiastes 12:12). His point was that fearing God and pleasing him are what bring true fulfillment.

"Spirits Dance in Paradise" by Beato Angelico

The Book of Life

The most commonly mentioned heavenly book is the Book of Life. It refers to the keeping of an account of those who are truly believers and those who are not. In Revelation, those whose names are found written in the Book of Life will escape the everlasting judgment. Most other heavenly books are related to the Book of Life in some way.

The House of the Archives

Jewish leaders once sent a request to the Persian king to search the royal archives for records that could clarify a local conflict. The king did, and found the relevant documents in "the house of the archives where the documents were stored." Every major empire had a vast bureaucracy supported by thousands of legal and administrative documents. Most excavations of ancient cities have uncovered royal archives with valuable troves of such documents.

A Bible for the Commoner

The New Testament was written in the language of the common person. This style is called *koine* Greek, meaning "common," "everyday." It contrasts sharply with the sophisticated and complex Greek of Athens, called Attic Greek. This meant that the New Testament could be read and understood by the vast majority of people throughout the Mediterranean world.

Athens

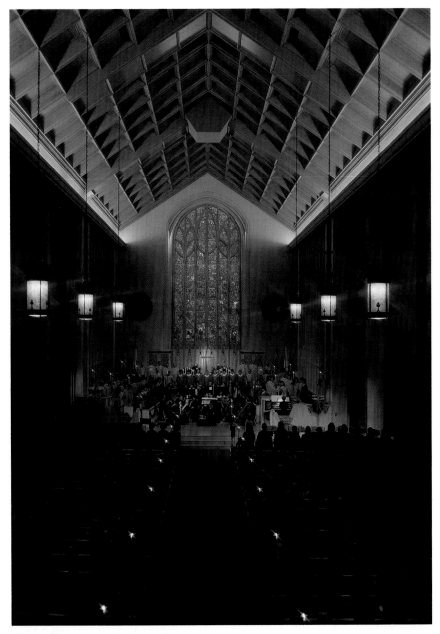

All Sins Are Forgiven!
Psalm 32 is a beautiful reflection on the joys of having one's sins forgiven. It uses no less than four words for sin in its opening lines: "Happy are those whose *transgression* is forgiven, whose *sin* is covered. Happy are those to whom the Lord imputes no *iniquity*, and in whose spirit there is no *deceit*." The variety of terms used creates the solid assurance that whatever the sin is, it is covered and forgiven.

Studying Torah and Shooting Arrows

The Hebrew verb that is related to the noun Torah is *yarah*, which means "to shoot an arrow." The relationship between the two is that the Torah points in the right direction, aims toward the mark of a right relationship with God. Interestingly enough, one of the major words for sin in Hebrew (*chata*) means "to miss the mark."

Familiar Greek Words

Many English words have their roots in Greek words used in the New Testament. *Theos* ("God") and *logos* ("word," "study") yields theology (the study of God). *Megalo* ("great") and *polis* ("city") yield megalopolis (huge metropolitan area). *Ekklesia* ("church") yields ecclesiastical (having to do with the church). *Anthropos* ("man") yields anthropology (the study of man). *Angelos* is "angel"; *ethnosis* is "nation"; *proselutos* is "proselyte"; *baptizo* is "baptize"; *meter* is "mother"; *pater* is "father."

99

Philistine pottery

Philistine Behavior

The word philistine has come to mean uncultured or boorish in English. This is because of the mostly negative presentation of the Philistines in the Bible, who were Israel's major enemy between 1150 to 1000 B.C. The Philistine culture, however, was fairly advanced in political organization and especially in the arts.

Stammering Barbarians

Our word "barbarian" comes from the Greek *barbaros*, which referred to a foreigner, someone speaking an unintelligible language. It is found in Romans 1:14, referring to non-Greeks. The word arose to imitate the way a foreign tongue sounded to Greek ears, a stammering, unknown sound. Originally, it had no insulting connotation at all.

What Is a Helpmate?

This usually refers to a wife, in her role as helper to her husband. The word has arisen from the King James Version's rendering of two Hebrew words in Genesis 2:18, where God says, "I will make [Adam] an help meet for him." However, "meet" in seventeenth-century English meant "appropriate," "fit for." So, helpmate was not originally a true word; modern versions usually translate the phrase "a helper fit for him."

A Biblical Airhead?

Jesus spoke about empty-headed people when he said, "Anyone who says to his brother 'Raca,' is answerable to the Sanhedrin" (Matthew 5:22). The Aramaic word is one of insult, related to the Hebrew term for empty. It means something like empty-headed one (airhead or blockhead).

"Sermon on the Mount" by James J. Tissot

The Salt Covenant

Salt was a seasoning to be offered with Israelite sacrifices, and covenants were sealed with sacrificial meals where salt was present. Since salt was also a preservative, a "salt covenant" symbolized eternity. This first referred to the holy offerings due the priests and Levites in perpetuity (Numbers 18:19), and later the eternal kingship that God had given David and his sons (2 Chronicles 13:5).

An Eye for an Eye

The penalties stated in Exodus 21:23–25 concerning an eye for an eye or a life for a life sound barbaric to many people today. However, the principle was a very humane one: Let the punishment fit the crime. In the ancient Near Eastern world, this limited the usual cycle of escalating retribution and revenge.

"Paul" by Peter Paul Rubens

Paul's Thorn in the Flesh

The Apostle Paul mentioned a "thorn in the flesh" that was given him to keep him from pride (2 Corinthians 12:7). He asked God three times about it, but it was never removed. Scholars have speculated almost endlessly about what it was. Suggestions include earaches, headaches, eye afflictions, epilepsy, hysteria, malaria, speech impediment, sexual lust, or human enemies. Unfortunately, we do not know what his problem was.

The Canaanites: Israel's Thorn in Its Sides

When Israel inherited the land of Canaan, one of its top priorities was to drive out the Canaanites, who worshiped many pagan gods. God repeatedly warned them of the dangers of mixing with them. At one point, he stated that they would be "as pricks in your eyes and thorns in your sides" (Numbers 33:55).

Canaanite Astarte statues

"Aurora" by Guido Reni

Chariots of the Sun

King Josiah removed the "horses that the kings of Judah had dedicated to the sun" from the entrance to the Temple, and he burned their "chariots of the sun" with fire as part of his great reform movement (2 Kings 23:11). Worship of the sun god was common in the ancient Near East, and several cultures depicted him as a charioteer riding across the sky pulling the sun behind him.

An Archaic Word: *Neesing*

Job 41 describes a creature called Leviathan that many scholars believe is the crocodile. Parts of the description make it sound like a dragon. Here is the King James Version of verse 18: "By his neesings a light doth shine." *Neesing* was the seventeenth-century word for "sneezing."

Apocalypse beast

666: The Number of the Beast

The beast's number is 666 (Revelation 13:18). This has led to endless speculation about the beast's identity. Some people have used various methods of assigning numbers to letters. Many early interpreters thought individual Roman emperors were being referred to. Irenaeus (and many modern interpreters) saw the number as symbolic of all evil. Being one digit short of the triple number of perfection—777—it symbolizes evil's perversion and falling short of the true standard of perfection.

Jesus and the U.S. Marines

The United States Marine Corps had a recruiting slogan that said they were looking for "a few good men." This is similar to Jesus' words about the relatively few people who actually would respond to his invitation to salvation—"many are called, but few are chosen" (Matthew 22:14). The major difference is that the Marines' invitation was selective, while Jesus' was inclusive.

From Dust To Dust

"Ashes to ashes, dust to dust" are words often spoken at the gravesite during a funeral. The term is adapted from God's words to Adam in Genesis 3:19, reminding him that he was formed out of the ground and would return there: "you are dust, and to dust you shall return."

Silver shekel

Thirty Pieces of Silver

The price paid to Judas for Jesus was 30 pieces of silver. This was a ridiculously low sum. In the Old Testament, this was the sum to be paid if a man's ox gored a slave. This reflects the low esteem in which Jesus was held by Judas and the Jewish leaders.

Faith, Hope, and Love

Paul's great reflections on love are found in 1 Corinthians 13. At the end of his discussion, he stresses that "faith, hope, and love" are the greatest of all gifts, but he concludes that "the greatest of these is love."

"Kiss of Judas"

Blood Money

When Judas Iscariot betrayed Jesus to the Jewish authorities, Judas was given 30 pieces of silver in payment. This has led to the phrase "blood money," which is money received in exchange for the life of a human being.

Swing Low, Sweet Chariot?

The old Negro spiritual by this title speaks (mistakenly) of the chariot that will take the believer home (to heaven). The image comes from 2 Kings 2:11, where Elijah was taken into heaven by a fiery chariot and fiery horses. However, the text actually says that Elijah was taken up in a whirlwind, not in the chariot itself.

Chariots of Fire

The Abomination of Desolation

Daniel 11 speaks of the rise of Antiochus Epiphanes, the ruler of the Seleucid Empire, and of his profaning of the Temple in Jerusalem in 168 B.C. He is a "contemptible person" (verse 21), and he will set up "an abomination of desolation" (verse 31). The books of 1 and 2 Maccabees detail this desecration. Jesus predicted that another "desolating sacrilege" would be set up in Jerusalem at the end of the age.

Jerusalem

Chariots of Fire

The Academy-Award-winning movie *Chariots of Fire* took its name from a biblical image, which was appropriate, since it was a story about a committed Christian runner. The image comes from 2 Kings 2:11, where a chariot of fire and horses of fire appeared and the prophet Elijah was taken up into heaven. Isaiah 66:15 also mentions the Lord coming angrily in chariots of fire to judge the earth.

Jordan River

Rolling Away in Gilgal

The first place the Israelites encamped in the land of Canaan after they had crossed the Jordan River was Gilgal. Here they circumcised all males, since they had neglected this practice in the wilderness. They named the site "Gilgal" in a word-play on the reproach of Egypt that was finally rolled away (Joshua 5:9). The Hebrew word for "to roll" is *galal*.

What or Where is *Sheol*?

The Hebrew term *sheol* occurs 65 times in the Old Testament, referring to the place of the dead. The King James Version translates it "hell" 31 times, the "grave" 31 times, and the "pit" 3 times. While it means merely the grave at times, sometimes it seems to refer more to a shadowy realm of the dead. The full-blown concept of hell as a place of punishment is not developed in the Old Testament.

Hell

This English word comes from an old Germanic word meaning "hidden place." The King James Version translates several words as hell: sheol, hades, and gehenna. The last of these is the most proper source for hell, however. In the New Testament, the idea of hell as eternal punishment is found in its full expression. It is accompanied by fiery imagery ("a lake of fire"), and its location is a nebulous place under the earth.

"Hell" by D. Bouts

115

❧ ANIMALS AND PLANTS ❧

"Baboons! But I Ordered Peacocks!"

Every three years, King Solomon's fleet of trading ships brought back many riches, including "baboons," according to the New International Version, or "peacocks," according to the New Revised Standard Version. The Hebrew word is either related to the Egyptian word for baboon or the Tamil (Indian) word for peacock.

A Whale of a Tale?

Contrary to popular belief, Jonah was probably not swallowed by a whale. Jonah's fateful journey was in the Mediterranean, where whales are rarely sighted today and may have been unknown in biblical times. The Bible merely mentions a "great fish" and a "large sea monster" as Jonah's seaworthy refuge.

"The Animals Entering the Ark" by Jacob Savery

Animals on the Ark

All the animals did not enter the ark two by two; some boarded the boat in parties of 14. These included all the birds and the clean animals that were approved for eating by Hebrew dietary law.

Biblical Animals

The Bible mentions dozens of animals, wild and domestic, in many different contexts. Almost 180 Hebrew terms exist for animals, and more than 50 Greek terms. Unfortunately, not all the terms can be identified with certainty, and many animals have become extinct since biblical times.

Unicorns in the Bible?

The King James Version of the Bible mentions unicorns nine times. The actual animal is the oryx, a magnificent white horselike creature with two long, straight horns. It was hunted almost to extinction in the nineteenth century. Today, it is slowly being restored in Israel by wildlife conservationists.

Dogs

In Israel, dogs ran loose and lived as scavengers. They were despised and considered unclean by the Israelites. Proverbs 26:11 mentions a dog returning to its vomit, and, in one gruesome episode, the wicked queen Jezebel's body was eaten by dogs in the street after her death. Some dogs were kept as sheepdogs though, and some may even have been household pets in some lands.

Camels

The camel is an ideal desert beast of burden, since it has an extraordinary ability to go long periods of time without water. Because of its ungainly looks, some people joke that it is a horse put together by committee. The camel was domesticated about 3000 B.C., but it was not commonly used until the twelfth century B.C. We get our word "camel" from the Hebrew word *gamal*.

Jezebel's death

Animals and Humans

Genesis 1 and 2 tell us that God created animals before humans, that he gave humans responsibility to be good stewards over the animals, and that Adam gave names to them. Originally, humans were vegetarians, but after Noah's flood, God gave animals for food as well. Animals served humans as sources of food, for transportation, in working the fields, as sacrificial animals, in the military, and as pets.

"Garden of Eden" by Jacob Bouttats

Donkeys

Donkeys are mentioned frequently in the Bible. The donkey was one of the basic possessions of the ordinary Hebrew family. It was used for powering machinery to grind corn, for pulling simple plows, and for riding. It was an unclean animal, and thus not to be eaten, although during a siege of Samaria, a donkey's head was sold for food at a very high price (2 Kings 6:25).

Cats

Cats are mentioned only in the apocryphal Letter of Jeremiah (verse 22). This verse speaks of bats, swallows, birds, and cats alighting with impunity on the heads of idols, which shows that the idols are not gods. Cats were sacred in Egypt, and their mummies were preserved by the thousands. They were domesticated in Egypt for catching rodents, since large-scale grain storage was practiced, but they were not kept in Palestine.

Balaam's Donkey

Balaam holds the dubious distinction of being the only biblical character to have had a conversation with a donkey. Balaam was an enigmatic Mesopotamian prophet and magician who was hired by Balak, an enemy of Israel, to curse Israel. On his way there, his donkey balked at going on because it saw an angel and was fearful. The donkey even spoke to Balaam about this, according to Numbers 22:28–30.

Balaam and his donkey meet the angel.

Kings and Donkeys

Several passages in the Old Testament speak of a king riding on a donkey. This is most striking in Zechariah 9:9, where it is prophesied that a king comes triumphant and victorious yet riding humbly on a donkey (and chariots and war horses are mentioned in the next verse). Jesus' entrance into Jerusalem on a donkey fulfilled this prophecy (Matthew 21:5). The use of a donkey instead of a horse emphasized the peaceful nature of the king.

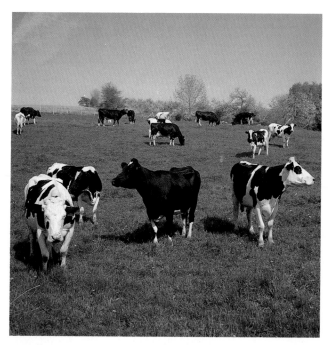

Cattle

Many different words were used to represent cattle, including herd, heifer, bull, calf, and ox. Cattle were kept in great numbers in biblical lands, and they were symbols of wealth. The cattle provided milk, meat, leather, manure (fuel for cooking), and horns, and they were also used as draft animals and for sacrifices.

Unequally Yoked Animals

It was common in ancient times (as well as modern times) to yoke an ox and a donkey together to pull a plow. However, the Mosaic Law prohibited this (Deuteronomy 22:10). While this may have been primarily for its moral lesson, it also was humane, since the two animals are not well matched for joint work.

Oxen

Several words in Hebrew are translated variously as cattle, bulls, oxen, etc. Oxen are castrated adult bulls. They were used in biblical lands as sacrificial animals, for plowing and other agricultural uses, and they provided hides and meat as well. They are thought to have originated with the wild ox, which many scholars think was the aurochs, an animal that is now extinct.

"Away in a Manger"

The Gospel of Luke mentions the manger into which Jesus was laid when he was born (Luke 2:7). Most scholars think this was a feeding trough for cattle. Excavations at Megiddo and Lachish, towns of the Old Testament period, have uncovered stone feeding troughs of this type. St. Jerome stated that Jesus' manger was made of mud or clay, which may be true given the scarcity of wood and the difficulty of hewing out stone.

"Adoration of the Shepherds" by Peter Paul Rubens

Bronze bull from Samaria

Sheep

Hebrew has some 12 different words for sheep, such as ram, lamb, ewe, and flock. This undoubtedly reflects the important place sheep had in Israelite life and economy in Old Testament times. Sheep were the most common animals to be sacrificed. Both the Old and New Testaments refer often to sheep symbolically as innocent, helpless, docile, or sacrificial animals. One of the best-known verses is in the beloved Psalm 23, which begins, "The Lord is my shepherd, I shall not want."

Bulls

Bulls were symbols of strength in most cultures in the ancient Near East. As such, they came to be objects of worship. Typically, the highest of the gods were represented as having bull-like features. Bulls adorned royal thrones, palaces, and temples. The Israelites fell prey to bull worship, building golden bull calves on at least two occasions.

122

❦ ANIMALS AND PLANTS ❦

Lambs

Lambs are almost exclusively symbolic in the Bible. They represented innocence and gentleness. God's care for his people was often expressed in terms of a shepherd watching over his lambs. Unblemished lambs were to be sacrificed for people's sins, and Jesus is called the Lamb of God, referring to his status as an innocent who was sacrificed for the world's sins.

Lice

The third plague on the Egyptians was the plague of lice, according to several Bible versions (some versions say maggots or gnats). Lice were a common problem in the ancient world, and the ancients fashioned beautiful combs to deal with the problem. Archaeologists have found the remains of lice and their eggs in combs at many sites.

Locusts

The eighth plague on Egypt was an incredible swarm of locusts, and the books of Joel and Revelation depict locusts as God's instruments of judgment. Even in modern times, swarms of locusts have darkened the skies and devastated areas up to 400 square miles.

Goats

Goats were kept for their milk, the meat of the kid, and for sacrificial purposes. Goatskins were used for carrying liquids, and the goat's long hair was used in making cloth. Seventy percent of the Bible's references to goats are as animals for sacrifice, although sheep were more commonly used. Jesus mentioned that all people would be separated into the sheep (favored) and the goats (condemned) at the final judgment.

123

Ceramic cult stand with serpents

Snakes: Threats to Life

Snakes are mentioned in the Bible mostly as symbols, usually as threats. Evil entered the world through Satan in the form of a snake (Genesis 3), and wicked people are often compared to snakes or their venom. The threat of great harm is often compared to a snakebite. The craftiness of snakes also is mentioned, as Jesus told his disciples to be wise as serpents and innocent as doves.

Dragons

Dragons are found in both the Old and New Testaments. In the Old Testament, the term is sometimes more accurately translated as serpent, but often it refers to the great monster of mythology. It is a symbol of evil. In Revelation 12, it is a symbol of Satan. Dragons are known from the literature and art of the ancient Near East as well.

Fish

Fish were an abundant source of food in all Bible lands. The Law of Moses (Deuteronomy 14:9,10) allowed eating "whatever has fins and scales" (most fish), but it prohibited eating whatever did not have these (thus excluding sharks, eels, and rays, and water mammals, reptiles, and invertebrates). The Israelites, as well as Jesus and his disciples, regularly ate fish.

❦ ANIMALS AND PLANTS ❦

Snake Handlers

Mark 16 states that just before Jesus returned to heaven, he told his followers that they would have new powers because of their faith: They would be able to cast out demons, speak in new languages, handle deadly snakes, and drink poison with no harm. Some eccentric Christian groups today, mainly in Appalachia, take this to mean that all Christians *must* do this, and they handle snakes and drink poisons as part of their religious rituals.

The Symbolism of Fish

Fish and fishing are mentioned symbolically many times in the Bible. Usually the imagery has to do with catching fish, whether with nets or otherwise. Amos' prophecy about Samaria's doom is jarring: "they shall take you away with hooks, even the last of you with fishhooks" (Amos 4:2). Jesus spoke of making his disciples "fishers of men" (Matthew 4:19). Deuteronomy 4:18 prohibited the making of any image of a fish.

Shekel coins

Saint Peter's Fish

Jesus told his disciple Peter to go fish in the Sea of Galilee, predicting that the first fish he caught would have a shekel coin in its mouth (Matthew 17:24–27). Peter was then to take this shekel and pay his and Jesus' taxes with it. The fish was probably the Tilapia, a fish commonly found in the Sea of Galilee. This fish has a large mouth in which it carries its eggs, and it is often called St. Peter's Fish.

125

Jesus' Sponge

Roman soldiers gave Jesus a drink from a sponge while he was on the cross. Sponges are marine animals whose skeletons provide the familiar sponge. The Roman writer Pliny states that it was standard practice for Roman soldiers to carry a sponge with them to use in getting themselves a drink, precisely in the way that the Gospels describe.

Hornets

Three times the Bible mentions that God sent swarming hornets ahead of the Israelites into the land of Canaan to drive out their enemies. Some scholars see this as a literal reference to hornets, while others see it as a symbol of Egypt, just as the fly and the bee are symbols of Egypt and Assyria in Isaiah 7:18. Others see it as a symbol of God's direct intervention, which paralized the enemy.

Bees

The Bible mentions bees a number of times. Twice the swarming habits of honeybees are mentioned: Psalm 118:12 says that "[The nations] surrounded me like bees," while Deuteronomy 1:44 mentions the Amorites chasing the Israelites like bees. Samson encountered a swarm of honeybees in the carcass of a lion (Judges 14:8). The Hebrew word for "bee" is *deborah*.

Scorpions

Scorpions are mentioned many times in the Bible, always as threats the Israelites faced or as symbols of great pain and hardship. Jesus appointed 70 followers to whom he gave authority to "tread upon serpents and scorpions...and nothing shall hurt you" (Luke 10:19).

Crocodile Wrestling

Job 41 tells of the crocodile's mighty power as follows: "Lay hands on him; think of the battle; you will not do it again!" (verse 8). It describes the crocodile's snout and skin this way: "Who can strip off his outer garment? Who can penetrate his coat of mail? Who can open the doors of his face? Round about his teeth is terror. His back is made of rows of shields...." (verses 13–15).

Crocodiles

Crocodiles were abundant in the Nile River in biblical times, although not elsewhere. An entire chapter in Job is devoted to describing the crocodile, called "Leviathan" (Job 41). The chapter contains a series of rhetorical questions to Job about what he can do to the awesome crocodile (answer: nothing). This makes the point that God created even this fearsome creature. The descriptions in this chapter are surprisingly detailed.

Ostriches

The ostrich was common in biblical lands, but today it is extinct there. It was used for food and for its feathers, and it is occasionally depicted in the art of Egypt and Assyria. Ornamental cups made from ostrich eggshells have been found in Assyrian graves from about 3000 B.C. Ostriches are described in considerable detail in Job 39:13–18, where their reputation for cruelty and stupidity is mentioned, as well as their blinding speed.

Birds

The Bible mentions some 50 types of birds. More than 350 species of birds are identified today in Palestine. Birds are included among sacrificial animals and among clean (edible) and unclean animals. They figure in numerous stories in the Bible (the doves and raven of Noah's ark). Their habits and nesting places are referred to often in prophetic and poetic literature.

Little green bee eater

Lizards

Leviticus 11:29–30 mentions several animals that are unclean, most of them reptiles related to the lizard. They include "the great lizard...the gecko, the land crocodile, the lizard, the sand lizard, and the chameleon." These all were among the "swarming things that swarm upon the earth." Lizards were (and are) common in Palestine.

Owls

No less than eight species of owls have been tentatively identified from the lists of unclean birds in Leviticus and Deuteronomy, including the eagle owl, short- and long-eared owls, wood owl, fisher owl, screech owl, little owl, and scops owl. The eagle owl is the world's largest, measuring up to 28 inches long. A beautiful sandy-colored desert variety is known from Palestine.

Fisher owl

Falcons

The falcon is a bird of prey. About ten species are known from Palestine. In Leviticus 11:14, falcons are mentioned as an abomination, not to be eaten. Job 28:7 speaks of their keen vision. One of the highest Egyptian gods was Horus, a falcon-god.

"Noah in the Ark" by Ditlev Blunk

Doves and Pigeons

Doves and pigeons were the most important birds in the Old Testament. They were used often in sacrifices. When pigeons were used, they were always "young pigeons" (see Leviticus 1:14). Noah sent out three doves from the ark to find land; the second brought back an olive leaf, a symbol of new life. Jesus talked about doves to symbolize guiltlessness when he said "be wise as serpents and innocent as doves" (Matthew 10:16).

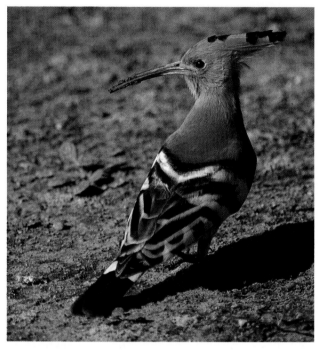

Hoopoes

The hoopoe is mentioned only twice, in the lists of abominations in Leviticus 11:19 and Deuteronomy 14:18. It is a beautiful bird, but it is filthy in its eating and nesting habits. Also, it was a sacred bird to the Egyptians. These facts probably account for its prohibition in Israel. It has spectacular plumage, including a fanlike crest. Its beak is long, thin, and curved.

Ravens

The raven is the largest member of the crow family, and it is first encountered in the story of Noah's flood (Genesis 8:7). It was one of the unclean animals (Leviticus 11:15). God's care for the raven was a symbol of his care for his people, and it also was a symbol of judgment and desolation.

Roosters

The common cock is mentioned once in the Old Testament, in Proverbs 30:31: "the strutting rooster." In the New Testament, Mark 13:35 mentions "cockcrow" as the signal for morning. The only other reference is to the cock that crowed when Peter denied Jesus.

Hens

Jesus used a tender image in describing God's concern for wayward Jerusalem: "How often would I have gathered your children together as a hen gathers her brood under her wings..." (Matthew 23:37). Otherwise, chickens are mentioned only perhaps in the provisions for Solomon's table ("fatted fowl" in 1 Kings 4:23) and at Nehemiah's table ("fowls...were prepared for me" in Nehemiah 5:18). They were not native to Palestine.

Jerusalem

Partridges

The partridge is mentioned only twice, once in a reference to hunting it in the mountains (1 Samuel 26:20), and once in Jeremiah 17:11, where it "gathers a brood which she did not hatch." The Hebrew word for partridge is *qore* ("one who calls"), referring to the distinctive sound it makes. Three species of partridge are known in Palestine, where it is the most common gamebird.

Crane mosaic from Tabgha

Cranes

The crane is a beautiful, large wading bird, with long neck, legs, and bill, similar to a heron. It is mentioned twice in the Bible. Isaiah 38:14 mentions its noisy call and Jeremiah 8:7 mentions its regular migrating habits.

Storks

Storks are large, beautiful birds, standing more than three feet tall. They were considered unclean, however (Leviticus 11:19), no doubt because they feed in muddy places and eat mostly mice, frogs, fish, and small birds. They too are migratory birds, as Jeremiah 8:7 indicates.

Quail

Quail are mentioned in connection with only one event in the Bible. When the Israelites were in the wilderness, God sent quail into the camp in the evening and the people collected them for food. Quail are small gamebirds that migrate, but they can only do so with the help of the wind. The Bible states that they did come in on the wind (Numbers 11:31).

Vultures

Hebrew and Greek each have only one word for vultures and eagles, since they are both large birds that fly high in the sky and are indistinguishable to the common person's eye. Both were (and are) common in Palestine. Proverbs 30:17 mentions being eaten by vultures and several other passages mention vultures circling overhead (Lamentations 4:19 and Matthew 24:28).

Eagles

Eagles are mentioned more often than any bird of prey in the Bible. They are impressive for their great size, strength, speed, and soaring abilities. They are usually mentioned in stirring words: "You have seen...how I [God] bore you on eagles' wings and brought you to myself" (Exodus 19:4). "They who wait for the Lord shall renew their strength, they shall mount up with wings like eagles...." (Isaiah 40:31).

Fowlers

Fowlers were people who hunted wild birds, which were very common in Bible lands. Fowlers supplied birds for use as caged pets, for food, and as sacrifices. They most commonly caught birds using nets and snares, but they also used decoy birds, bows and arrows, slings, and throw-sticks. The references to fowlers in the Old Testament are metaphorical, usually speaking of their snares.

"Daniel in the Lions' Den" by Briton Riviere

The Lions' Den

The lions' den was a pit or trench in which lions were kept. It is mentioned in the story of Daniel, who was thrown there when he refused to stop praying toward Jerusalem (Daniel 6:16–24). When he was vindicated, his false accusers and their families were themselves thrown in the den and devoured by the lions. This practice was not known otherwise in the ancient Near East, but Job 38:39,40 does speak of lions crouching in their dens.

Lion seal
from Megiddo

Satyrs?

Satyrs in classical mythology were forest gods, half man and half goat. The Revised Standard Version translates the Hebrew term *sha ir* as "satyrs" several times, while the New Revised Standard Version renders it "goat-demons" (Isaiah 13:21 and 34:14). The references probably refer to a pagan deity with the form of a goat that lured the Israelites to worship it (Leviticus 17:7). Usually the Hebrew term means "hairy one" or "male goat."

Lions in the Ancient Near East

Lions were a favorite of kings. The Persian king kept lions in captivity during Daniel's day. In Egypt, lions were trained to help in the hunt, and Ramses II was said to have kept a tame lion that went with him into battle. The Assyrian kings liked to hunt lions. In Roman times, lions were used in sporting events in which they fought each other, bears, and gladiators. Christians also were ordered thrown to the lions by some emperors.

136

Gazelles

The gazelle is a type of antelope whose horns differ from those of the deer. The gazelle has horns that are hollow and do not branch. They are mentioned in the Bible for their speed and their beauty, and Isaiah 13:14 mentions the frightened "hunted gazelle."

Deer

Several different words for deer are found in the Bible. The "hart" is probably the roe deer. The male of the species weighs up to 300 pounds and has six-pronged antlers. It is not well suited for desert living, which is reflected in Psalm 42:1: "As the hart pants for streams of water...." The Bible usually mentions deer metaphorically, referring often to their graceful running and leaping abilities.

Horses

Horses were common in biblical lands. They are mentioned more than 140 times in Scripture. In Old Testament times, horses were held by royalty, and they were a symbol of royalty and human power. In Israel, kings were not to accumulate horses, but to leave military matters to God. David kept a few horses after one battle, but his son Absalom was able to capture them during his revolt against his father.

❧ ANIMALS AND PLANTS ❧

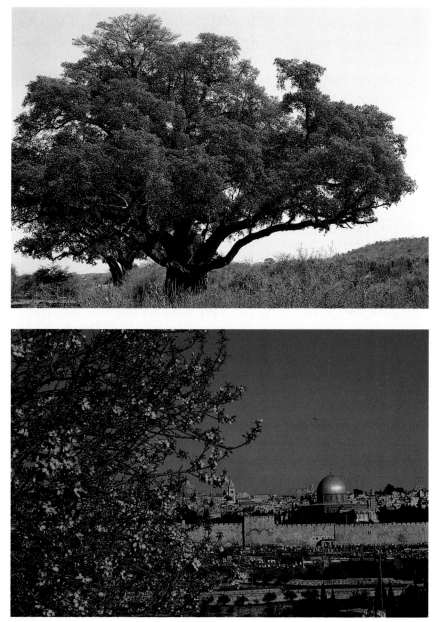

Almond trees in blossom outside Jerusalem

Sycamore Trees

The prophet Amos was a "dresser of sycamore trees" by profession (Amos 7:14). The figs of the sycamore tree require cutting open with a knife point at a certain stage to help in the ripening process, and Amos did this. Branches of the sycamore tree are strong and wide-spreading, and Zacchaeus climbed such a tree in order to see Jesus better (Luke 19:4).

Willow Trees

The willow tree is mentioned several times in the Bible. The true willow was a small shrub or tree growing near water, and it flourished in the Jordan Valley. Psalm 137:2 mentions that the Jewish exiles in Babylon hung their harps on the willows there, but this tree was probably a variety of the aspen or poplar tree, such as the tall Euphrates aspen.

Almond Trees

Joseph's father, Jacob, gave Joseph's brothers a present of rare delicacies that included almonds to take to their brother (Genesis 43:11). The tree's blooming in late January is a sign that spring is coming. Almonds served as models for the cups of the golden lampstand in the Tabernacle.

Aaron's Rod

Moses' brother Aaron, the high priest, had a very interesting rod. On one occasion, it turned into a snake that devoured the Egyptian magicians' rods/snakes (Exodus 7:12). On another occasion, it sprouted buds, blossoms, and almonds overnight; this was in a contest with the rebellious people concerning priestly authority (Numbers 17:8). This rod was kept in the Ark of the Covenant (Hebrews 9:4).

Ark of the Covenant

Thistles and Thorns

More than 20 words in the Bible describe thistles, thorns, brambles, and other prickly plants. They are mainly mentioned symbolically, when talking about fruitlessness or worthlessness. Abimelech, a ruthless pretender to the throne in early Israel, is compared to the lowly bramble. Jesus told a parable of thorns choking off seeds, comparing this to the snuffing out of faith in some new believers' lives.

Herbs and Spices

The Bible mentions about 15 to 20 herbs and spices, not all of which can be precisely identified. Some—such as cinnamon, aromatic cane, stacte, galbanum, and frankincense—were used to make sweet-smelling incense for religious purposes. Others—such as mint, dill, cumin, cinnamon, onions, and garlic—were used in preparing food. Still others—such as cassia, aloes, and spikenard—were used for cosmetics and medicines.

The Olive Branch

The olive branch has become an international symbol of peace and good will. This imagery comes from its association with the dove and the story of Noah, where a dove released from the ark returned with an olive branch in its beak (Genesis 8:11).

The Rose of Sharon

The Song of Solomon compares a man's lover to the "rose of Sharon." It was not a rose as we know it today, but probably a tulip of some kind, either the *Tulipa montana*, which grows in the mountains, or the *Tulipa sharonensis*, which grows on the Plain of Sharon.

Sweet Cane

Isaiah 43:24 mentions sweet cane. A wild cane is found throughout Palestine, but most scholars think this refers to the sugar cane. Honey was the most important sweetener in Old Testament times, but this cane was probably chewed or used to sweeten drinks and food.

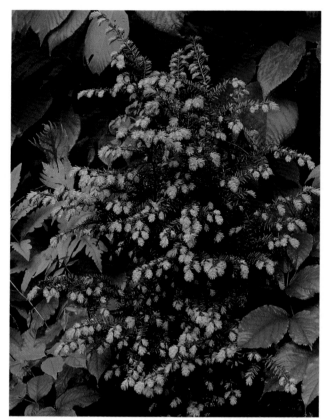

Hemlock

Hemlock and Wormwood

The King James Version mentions hemlock twice, but modern versions translate the word in question as "poisonous weed" or "wormwood." Wormwood is mentioned several times in the Old and New Testaments—it was known for its bitter, unpleasant taste. It came to symbolize sorrow, tragedy, and even cruelty.

Lilies

The Bible mentions lilies many times, but the term probably refers to different plants in different cases. Carved lilies (probably water lilies) were part of the Temple's decorations. The lilies of the field that Jesus mentioned were probably one of the colorful Palestinian wildflowers, either the poppy anemone, the white daisy, or the crown marguerite.

C. S. Lewis's Wormwood

In C. S. Lewis's fictional book *The Screwtape Letters*, about the correspondence between two devils, one devil is named Wormwood. His job is to poison the mind of the human being assigned to him. This imagery is taken from Revelation 8:8–11 where a star named Wormwood fell from heaven and poisoned the waters on earth.

Wormwood in Palestine

❧ TEMPLES AND SYNAGOGUES ❧

"Christ Drivi

A Priest

A beautifu
pomegran:
inscription
Jerusalem
eighth cen
inscription
Jerusalem
It was pro
scepter, oi
decoration

Personification of Spring mosaic from the Hammath Tiberias synagogue

Synagogue Mosaics

Synagogues have always been beautifully constructed. Many early synagogues had spectacular mosaics laid out on the floor, some covering the entire synagogue compound. These were intricately done, with thousands of small stones, and even their brilliant colors have been preserved.

The Temple

The Temple in Jerusalem was a magnificent building. Solomon had it built in about 960 B.C., but it was completely destroyed by the Babylonians in 586 B.C. The Persians allowed the Jews to rebuild it in 516 B.C. Around the time of Jesus, many additions were made to it by King Herod and others, but it was destroyed by the Romans a short time later, in A.D. 70. Today, the Islamic Dome of the Rock stands were the Temple once stood.

Dome of the Rock

Detail of Ark of the Covenant from Capernaum

A Perfect Cube

The Temple was carefully planned, including the details of its dimensions. It was an impressive structure, some 90 feet long, 45 feet wide, and 3 stories high. The innermost room, the Holy of Holies (or Most Holy Place), was where the Ark of the Covenant resided, symbolizing God's very presence. The Ark's dimensions formed a perfect cube.

Kidron Va...

The P...
the T...

A pries...
beginni...
Recent...
of an a...
Mount ...

The Ark of the Covenant

The Ark was Israel's most holy object. It was an ornate box made of acacia wood, overlaid with gold, and topped with a golden mercy seat flanked by two winged cherubs. It served as God's throne or footstool on earth, and it contained the tablets of the Ten Commandments, a pot of manna, and Aaron's rod. It was kept in the Most Holy Place of the Tabernacle and the Temple, but it was destroyed by the Babylonians in 586 B.C.

"The Seven Trumpets of Jericho" by James J. Tissot

No Cupids Here

Cherubim, or cherubs, were winged creatures found in the Tabernacle and Temple. Two small cherubim flanked the mercy seat of the Ark, two large ones flanked the Ark itself in the Temple, and cherubim were also woven into the fabric of the Tabernacle and its great veil. Many artistic representations of cherubs survive from the ancient Near East, usually having some animallike features, such as the body of a lion.

The Seven-Branched Lampstand

The Tabernacle and the Temple had a seven-branched lampstand (*menorah*) for light. A picture of it appears on the Arch of Titus in Rome as it was being carried away after the Temple's destruction in A.D. 70. The Talmud prohibited the making of any seven-branched menorahs outside the Temple.

Solomon's Temple

Gold, Gold, Gold

Much gold was used in Solomon's Temple. The interior faces of the stone walls were covered with fine wood and then overlaid with gold. We are told that the weight of gold coming in annually during Solomon's reign was 666 talents, or almost 50,000 pounds (1 Kings 10:14). In today's dollars, that would be worth almost $2.5 billion. Indeed, gold was so plentiful during Solomon's reign that silver was considered almost worthless.

A Quiet Construction Site

The Temple site was so holy that the raw building materials, including the huge stone blocks for the foundations and the walls, were prepared away from the site, and then brought to be installed in place. No tools—hammers, axes, or any iron tools—were heard on location, so that even the sounds of construction could not desecrate the site.

Pillars of Solomon's Temple shown on the cloth that covers the ark in a synagogue.

Bronze Pillars With Funny Names

The Temple had two tall free-standing bronze pillars at its entrance. Both had decorated bowls (possibly fire bowls) on top. The pillars stood more than 30 feet high, and both had names: *Jachin*, meaning "(God) will establish," and *Boaz*, meaning "in him is strength." When the Babylonians destroyed the Temple, they took these away with them for the valuable metal.

153

❧ WORSHIP AND RELIGIOUS PRACTICES ❧

"He Turned Their Waters Into Blood" by Erastus S. Field

Passover: Festival of Remembrance

Passover, or the Feast of Unleavened Bread, was a spring festival associated with the barley harvest. It commemorated the Israelites' flight from Egypt, when God's angel of death passed over and spared the Israelites (but not the Egyptians), and when the Israelites fled so quickly that they had no time to let their bread rise.

Biblical Festivals

The Mosaic Law established seven festivals. Three of these were great pilgrimage festivals that were related to the agricultural calendar: the feasts of Passover, Pentecost, and Tabernacles. The two high holy days—the Day of Atonement and New Year's Day—and two days of rest—the weekly Sabbath and the monthly New Moon festival—completed the festivals. The festivals of Purim and Hanukkah arose later.

"Pentecost" by Vasari

Pentecost: Early Harvest Feast

This feast was so named because it comes 50 days after the first sabbath of Passover—*pent* means 50. It is also known as the Feast of Weeks, First Fruits, or Harvest. It was a spring festival celebrating the completion of the grain harvest. Acts 2 tells us that Christians received the Holy Spirit on the day of Pentecost and spoke in languages not their own. Today, Pentecostals are Christians who practice speaking in tongues.

The Feast of Trumpets: New Year's Day?

A solemn day of rest, memorials, and sacrifices was set aside on the new moon of the seventh month and trumpets were blown on this day. In post-biblical times, it came to be associated with the New Year, the *Rosh Hashanah*, celebrated in the fall.

Sukkahs on an apartment building

Feast of Tabernacles: Fall Harvest Festival

This was also known as the Feast of Ingathering or Booths, and it was the greatest of the festivals. For seven days, the Israelites lived in booths or temporary shelters made out of branches and the harvest's fruit, to remind them of their desert accommodations and God's protection when they left Egypt. Even today, many Jews still erect ceremonial *sukkahs* (booths) in their backyards.

Blowing the shofar

New moon

Hanukkah: Festival of Dedication

The festival of *Hanukkah* (or "Dedication" mentioned in John 10:22) celebrates the rededication of the Temple in 164 B.C. after its desecration by Greeks. The festival, also called the Festival of Lights, lasts for eight days. According to the Talmud, the Jews found a lamp in the Temple with a one-day supply of oil, but it stayed miraculously lit for eight days of celebration. Today, the festival serves as an occasion for remembering and thanksgiving.

The New Moon Festival: A Monthly "Sabbath"

A monthly festival of rest, special sacrifices, and blowing of trumpets was observed at the new moon. The prophet Amos denounced greedy merchants who could not wait until the New Moon Festival was over so they could get back to their dishonest business practices. The new moon of the seventh month was set aside as a special day, known as the Feast of Trumpets.

The Day of Atonement: Erasing Sin

This was an annual day in the fall for fasting and rest (not feasting), and atoning for the nation's sins. This included careful cleansing of the high priest, the Tabernacle itself, and the people. Many offerings were sacrificed. It remains a high holy day for Jews today and is called Yom Kippur.

Lighting Hanukkah candles

Purim celebration

Purim scroll

Purim: Reversal of Anti-Semitism

Purim is the joyful festival in the Book of Esther, ordered by Mordechai to celebrate the Jews' great reversal of fortune. The Jews had been under an edict of death, but not only did they escape death, but they were also able to kill their enemies. The events show an early example of the many tragic, state-sponsored persecutions that have been directed against Jews.

The Sabbath: Day of Rest

The seventh day of the week was a day of rest, because God had rested from creating the world on the seventh day. The Jewish Talmud identified 39 main categories of work that were to be avoided on the Sabbath and devoted one lengthy part to spelling out how the Sabbath was to be observed and not profaned. Still today, Sabbath celebration begins at sundown on Friday evening, when Jewish families gather for a special meal. On Saturday morning, they go to the synagogue, and the rest of the day is spent resting, eating, and reading the Bible. The Hasidim liked this day so much they called it "Princess Sabbath."

Sabbath toast

God creates Eve.

Sabbath Breaking

The Sabbath day was very important. Not only could people rest and be refreshed, but they were reminded of God's great creation (Exodus 20:11). If people defiantly disobeyed God and worked on this day, the penalty was death (Exodus 31:15 and 35:2). Once, a man found gathering wood on the Sabbath was stoned to death (Numbers 15:32–36).

The Jubilee Year

The jubilee year was to come after seven sabbatical years, or every fiftieth year (Leviticus 25). It was a sabbatical year for the land (thus allowing two fallow years) and also a year when all lands would revert to their original owners. Also, anyone who had sold himself into service (because of debts) would regain his freedom. The idea was noble, but there is no record that either the sabbatical or jubilee years were ever actually observed.

The Sabbatical Year: A Humanitarian Policy

The Law provided for the land to lie unplanted every seventh year (Exodus 23 and Leviticus 25). This corresponded to the pattern of a weekly Sabbath for people and it allowed the land needed time to rest. More importantly, whatever grew in the fields was to be left for the poor and marginal members of society. Furthermore, debts were to be canceled in the seventh year, allowing people a fresh start (Deuteronomy 15).

Carrot harvest

163

Dreams

Interpretation of dreams was an important means of discerning the will of God in biblical times. Every ancient king retained court wise men to interpret dreams. Joseph and Daniel are the best-known dream interpreters in the Bible. Daniel was even required to tell the Babylonian king what the king had dreamed, and then interpret it for him.

Aranic incantation bowls

Sympathetic Magic

Almost 4,000 years ago, the Egyptians made pottery bowls and figurines upon which they would write the names of their enemies (called Execration Texts). They would then smash these items to pieces, hoping that this would induce their gods to crush these enemies for them.

Pharaoh's dream

Ecstatic Frenzies

The Bible mentions some prophets practicing a form of prophecy in something like an ecstatic frenzy, accompanied by noisy musical instruments (see especially 1 Samuel 10:5–13). This phenomenon was well known throughout the ancient Near East. One ancient Mesopotamian text speaks of the ravings of a *mahhu* (this was the Assyro-Babylonian title for the ecstatic prophets) as follows: "I am smitten down like a *mahhu*. That which I do not know, I bring forth."

"Saul Prophesying" by James J. Tissot

The Evil Eye

The Hebrew term for evil eye in the Old Testament means "a miserly, grudging, or envious look." However, outside the Bible, it reflects a widespread ancient belief that an envious or hostile glance by someone with special powers could cause harm. This belief is found in post-biblical Judaism as well.

Lilith, the Queen of Demons

This creature is mentioned only once in the Bible, in Isaiah 34:14; she is included among the creatures of deserted places. In rabbinic literature, she is an evil night creature with wings and long flowing hair. According to legend, she was Adam's first wife, but she was sent away because she demanded full equality with him. She took her revenge by trying to kill all newborn babies.

Laws of Cleanness and Uncleanness

The Israelite ceremonial law went to great lengths to distinguish between the realms of the clean and the unclean, and to prescribe rituals of cleansing. Sources of uncleanness included unclean animals, bodily emissions, various skin diseases (especially leprosy), and corpses. The basic purpose was to remind the Israelites of the great gap between them and God. The people needed to prepare themselves to meet with God, and they needed to do so properly and reverently.

Magic eye on an Egyptian house

Ritual bath (mikveh) at Herod's palace

Clean and Unclean Animals

Unclean animals were determined by several criteria. The two most important were hygiene and pagan practices. Unhygienic animals were scavengers and birds of prey, since they feed on rotting flesh. Pigs and scaleless fish were also unclean. Animals used in pagan worship or in witchcraft were unclean, such as pigs, fish, dogs, mice, hare, and various insects. Animals that were not typical of their class were also unclean.

The Red Heifer

An important means of purification in Israel involved killing an unblemished red heifer, one that had never been yoked. It was burned outside the camp along with aromatic woods, and then the ashes were mixed with water. Anyone who had become ritually unclean could wash in this water and be purified. The red color probably was chosen as a reminder of blood.

Samson

What was a Nazirite?

Nazirites were people—man, woman, or slave—who took special, voluntary vows to "separate themselves to the Lord" (Numbers 6:2). The vow included not drinking wine, not cutting one's hair, and not going near a dead body. Samson, Samuel, and John the Baptist were life-long Nazirites, dedicated by their parents (although Samson violated all of the vows). The Apostle Paul took a short-term Nazirite vow.

168

"A Sacrifice" by Knupfer

The Body and Blood of Christ

Christians celebrate the sacrificial death of Christ by eating and drinking bread and wine. The broken bread symbolizes Christ's broken body and the wine symbolizes his shed blood. Some Christians believe that these elements actually become the body and blood of Christ when a priest blesses them during the ceremony of the Eucharist (or mass).

Blood

Blood represented life in the Bible, and shed blood represented death. The sacrifice for sin required the shedding of blood. This was true whether the victim was an innocent animal or the ultimate sacrificial lamb, Jesus. Because of its special significance, Jews were to drain blood from meat before eating it. This is required for a kosher diet.

The Avenger of Blood

In many ancient societies, the relative of someone who was killed had the right to take vengeance for the death. Cain feared for his life because of this when he killed Abel. The Law of Moses accommodated this practice, but carefully regulated it. The Law distinguishes between accidental and deliberate homicide, provides cities of refuge, and requires the approval of the council of elders with two testifying witnesses before vengeance can be taken.

"Cain Kills Abel" by Tintoretto

"The Last Supper" from the Ingeburg Psalter of Denmark

The Holy Grail

This was the cup supposedly used by Jesus at the Last Supper with his disciples. It became the subject of many legends in the Middle Ages. At King Arthur's Round Table, an empty seat was reserved for the knight who found the Grail. In the early twentieth century, an ancient silver cup (known as the Chalice of Antioch) was publicized as being the Holy Grail, but it is usually dated no earlier than the fourth century A.D.

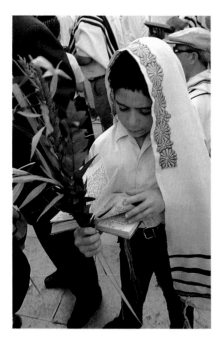

Palm Sunday

In Christian tradition, the Sunday before Easter has come to be known as Palm Sunday. This was because people welcomed Jesus into Jerusalem by spreading leafy branches on the road before his donkey as he was entering the city at the time of Passover (in the spring). The cutting of palm branches was usually practiced in the fall, at the Festival of Tabernacles, as part of the construction of the booths (Leviticus 23:40–42).

Palm Branch Waving

The four types of branches mentioned in Leviticus 23:40, which included palm branches, were to be held in one's hands during the reciting of the Hallel (Psalms 113–118), according to later Jewish custom. The palm branches were to be shaken three times in each direction of the four corners of the earth, symbolizing the abundance that comes from God in heaven.

Palm Sunday

Pilate's Hand Washing

The Roman governor Pilate washed his hands at Jesus' arraignment to symbolize his withdrawal from responsibility for whatever might happen to Jesus (Matthew 27:24). This practice was not new to him; undoubtedly it was a widespread custom. The Old Testament has many examples of ritual hand washing to symbolize innocence (Psalm 26:6 and Deuteronomy 21:6–8).

"Pilate Washing His Hands" by Rembrandt

Foot Washing

Since people wore open sandals and traveled dusty roads in Bible lands, their feet had to be washed frequently. This is mentioned several times in the Old Testament (see Genesis 18:4). Not washing one's feet was a sign of mourning (2 Samuel 19:24). It was considered to be the work of a menial slave, but Jesus washed his Disciples' feet in order to emphasize the necessity of serving others (John 13). The practice persists today in some Christian groups as a rite of worship.

"Christ Washes the Disciples' Feet" from the Ingeburg Psalter of Denmark

Hand Washing in Judaism

Ritual cleansing of the entire body was important in the Old Testament, but in Judaism the practice of ritual hand washing attained prominence. Jews washed their hands before and after meals, along with saying a prayer of blessing. They also washed their hands on other occasions, such as when getting out of bed or before offering daily prayers. This naturally resulted in good hygienic habits.

❧ WORSHIP AND RELIGIOUS PRACTICES ❧

The Tabernacle

What Was the Tent of Meeting?

In most cases, this was another term for the Tabernacle. Its name indicates that it was a place where people could meet God. But there was also a separate tent called the "tent of meeting" (Exodus 33:7). This was one that Moses used to pitch outside of the camp, where he and the people could also meet God. It was a temporary tent during the Israelites' days in the wilderness, and it was not known later in Israel's history.

Sacred Places

Besides the Temple and the Tabernacle, there were certain other places where people could go to speak with priests. There was a temple of the Lord at Shiloh before Solomon's Temple was built (1 Samuel 1). People also met at different times at Shechem, Bethel, Mizpah, Mounts Ebal and Gerizim, and many other places to worship God.

Mount Gerizim

The Horns of the Altar

The altar of burnt offering was to have four horns (like the pointed horns of an animal such as a bull), one on each corner. These functioned as the ultimate place of refuge or security, since we see two men in danger of their lives desperately clinging to them for protection (1 Kings 1–2). When the prophet Amos announced that even the horns of the altar at Bethel would be cut off, he was saying that there was no more escape for that wicked city.

Horned altars from Megiddo

176

High place at Gezer

High Places: Places of False Worship

The high places were sites of pagan, Canaanite worship that the Israelites often went to. The Israelites also built new high places of their own. The high places usually were on a hill, and they had an altar for sacrifices. The Israelite and Judean kings were continually condemned for tolerating or encouraging worship at these. Even many of the good kings "did right in the eyes of the Lord, but [they] did not remove the high places." Archaeology has revealed two rival Israelite temples, one at Arad (in southern Judah) and one at Elephantine (on the Nile River). In addition, a sanctuary was built at Bethel (Amos 7).

Yahweh the Bull?

The Bible prohibited any pictorial representations of God, but a valuable find in the middle 1970s in the Sinai Desert was a depiction of God as a bull on fragments of a storage jar. An inscription above his head reads "I bless you by Yahweh of Samaria and by his asherah." This is a dramatic example of the religious borrowing that was common in Israel and that the biblical prophets warned against.

Illustration of clay fragment

Clay fragment that depicts God as a bull.

Yahweh and His Asherah

The picture of Yahweh as a bull also has an Egyptian god standing next to him, and a seated lyre player, who probably represented his Asherah (the Canaanite goddess linked to Baal). If so, then this is an even more dramatic example of religious borrowing, by which Yahweh was given a wife or consort by some Israelites.

❧ WORSHIP AND RELIGIOUS PRACTICES ❧

The Luck of the Draw

Many important decisions in biblical times were made by drawing lots. The sacrificial goat on the Day of Atonement was chosen by lot, and the promised land was apportioned by lot. Achan was revealed by lot as the man responsible for Israel's defeat at Ai, and Saul was chosen Israel's first king by lot. In the New Testament, soldiers cast lots for Jesus' garments, and the disciple who replaced Judas Iscariot was selected by lot.

Bones used as lots

Assyrian lot

The Queen of Heaven

Some Jews of Jeremiah's day in Judah and in Egypt worshiped an astral goddess known as the "queen of heaven." They baked cakes for her and burned incense to her. This goddess was probably the Assyrian and Babylonian fertility goddess Ishtar (the Canaanite Astarte, associated with the planet Venus), or the Canaanite goddess Anath (who is called "the queen of heaven, the mistress of the gods" in an Egyptian text).

Ishtar

Jeremiah

Marduk: Babylonian High God

In the Law Code of Hammurabi, the god Marduk is accorded the highest status among the gods, taking over from Enlil. He retained this position until after the time of Christ. He was appealed to by an endless succession of Babylonian and Assyrian kings over the centuries. Jeremiah mentions Merodach's (Marduk's) shame in a prophecy predicting the downfall of Babylon (Jeremiah 50:2).

178

Bronze Calf at Ashkelon

In 1990, a small bronze calf with traces of silver overleaf was found at Ashkelon, dating before 1550 B.C. It was less than four inches long and four inches high, and it was housed in a small cylindrical clay shrine with a small doorway. It served as an object of worship for the Canaanites who lived at Ashkelon, and it recalls the golden calf incident at Mount Sinai. Early press reports mistakenly called this figurine a golden calf.

Baal: Canaanite High God

Baal was the god of the storms (and fertility), bringing rain and productivity to the land. He was the highest of the Canaanite gods. His cult posed a greater threat to true worship in Israel than did any other cult, since the Israelites lived in closest contact with the Canaanites. King Ahab of Israel gave the first official sanction to the worship of Baal, an action that the prophet Elijah vigorously denounced.

Ashkelon calf

The Prophets of Baal

Baal

Elijah and the Prophets of Baal

The prophet Elijah had a dramatic confrontation with 400 prophets of Baal, the Canaanite deity, on Mt. Carmel following a long drought. Elijah was able to call down fire from heaven, following which it began to rain. Baal's reputation was severely damaged because he had not brought fire or changed the weather, despite his prophets' desperate pleas.

179

Christ resists Satan.

Roman road

The Temptation of Christ

The Book of Hebrews states that Jesus, even though he was God, was tempted to sin just as we are, but he was able to resist the temptation (4:15). This is part of an argument that he identifies with our struggles. The Bible says nothing about the normal temptations he probably faced growing up, but it does record the three temptations by Satan at the beginning of his public ministry (Matthew 4).

The Seven Deadly Sins

This is the term used in the Middle Ages to refer to the seven sins thought to lead to damnation. They are pride, covetousness (greed), lust, anger, gluttony, envy, and sloth (laziness).

Going the Extra Mile

In the Sermon on the Mount, Jesus spoke repeatedly about going beyond the minimal requirements of law or social courtesy in order to show true generosity of spirit. One vivid illustration was when he said "if any one forces you to go one mile, go with him two miles" (Matthew 5:41). This referred to a detested Roman practice of forcing civilians into the service of carrying military baggage for a prescribed distance, one Roman mile.

Water Baptism

Baptism with water was an integral part of the early Christians' lives. Jesus himself was baptized. Peter preached, "Repent, and be baptized...for the forgiveness of your sins" (Acts 2:38). Jewish custom stressed ritual washings, but baptism was really a Christian development. Most early baptisms were by water immersion, but pouring and sprinkling developed as alternate modes. The meaning assigned to baptism differs among different Christian groups.

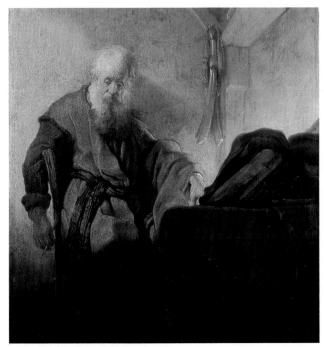

"Saint Paul in Prison" by Rembrandt

Pentecost

The Baptism of the Holy Spirit

Several times Jesus prophesied about a baptism that would be from the Holy Spirit after he had left the earth. John the Baptist stated that his baptism was with water, but Jesus' was different: "he will baptize you with the Holy Spirit and with fire" (Matthew 3:11). Paul spoke of all believers being "baptized into one body" by one Spirit (1 Corinthians 12:13). This means that Christians would be filled and covered with the Spirit as they were covered by water in baptism.

Paul and Adoption

Adoption was common in Greek and Roman cultures. Under Roman law, the adoptee left his old status and entered into a new relationship as a son to his new father. His old debts were canceled and he started a new life. He had all the rights and responsibilities of any natural-born children. Paul used this beautiful imagery to portray what happens to believers: They are adopted into God's family as his own children (Romans 8).

Christian Head Coverings

Christian tradition was the opposite of Jewish tradition, following Greek custom: Men's heads were not to be covered during worship (1 Corinthians 11:4). Indeed, this was a sign of dishonor to God. Women, however, were to have their heads covered as a sign of honor (11:5,6). Scholars disagree whether Paul meant that a woman's head covering was to be a veil or shawl, or merely long hair.

Jewish Head Coverings

Jewish males traditionally have worn a skull cap for prayer and meals. This was regarded in the Talmud as a sign of reverence for God. Indeed, the Talmud indicates that rabbis did not walk even four steps with their heads uncovered. This custom may have arisen from the priests' head covering mentioned in Exodus 28:37–39.

"My word is as good as gold!"

Most people know that Esau sold his birthright to his brother Jacob for a bowl of stew. Jacob then tricked his father into pronouncing the blessing on him. When the trick was discovered, Isaac was unable to revoke it. Isaac was bound to his oath, and so he could only pronounce a very vague, generic blessing on Esau.

"Let your yea be yea."

This expression comes from Jesus' words in the Sermon on the Mount, when he stated that people should not swear falsely, nor should they take any oaths by heaven or by Jerusalem or by anything else. A simple yes or no should be binding. The King James Version says "let your communication be, Yea, yea; Nay, nay" (Matthew 5:37).

"Isaac Blessing Jacob" by Gerbrandt van den Eeckhout

"The Sermon on the Mount and Healing the Leper" by Rosselli Cosimo

"My word is my honor!"

The importance of a spoken oath is indicated in a parallel from ancient Nuzi. In one court document, a spoken will is being contested in court. However, the court upholds the validity of the will, even though it was not written down. This is especially remarkable since it is found in a society in which written records have been found by the thousands!

"Saint Michael, the Archangel" by Guido Reni

The Worm and the Toothache

One of the best-known incantations used in ancient Babylonia is one intended to rid the sufferer of a toothache. It tells of how the worm had asked Shamash, the sun god, where he could dwell. He asked to be allowed to dwell in the gums of people and live off their blood. The text then curses the worm for this. The sufferer was to repeat the curse three times, in hope of relieving the pain.

Rabbinic Keys

In rabbinic literature, giving keys symbolized the granting of authority. Rabbi Akiva stated that God would give the angels Michael and Gabriel the keys to open the 40,000 gates to hell. Another Jewish belief held that God held four keys in his hand: the keys to rain, conception, resuscitation of the dead, and crops.

Ring is a Roman period house key.

Roman period key

The Key of David

Eliakim was made the grand vizier, or steward, over the household of King Hezekiah (Isaiah 22:15–25). He was given "the key of the house of David" to wear on his shoulder. This symbolized his exclusive authority to grant access to the king. This image is picked up in Revelation 3:7, where Christ now has "the key of David," and he alone opens the door of access to God.

Peter's Keys

Jesus told Peter that "I will give you the keys of the kingdom of heaven, and whatever you bind on earth shall be bound in heaven" (Matthew 16:19). This was a statement of the authority he received. The Roman Catholic tradition has held that this authority was exclusively Peter's, and, through him, the Church's. Protestant traditions have held that Peter represents the Apostles, and the authority refers to the wider apostolic message and mission.

"Christ's Charge to Peter" by Peter Paul Rubens

❧ Everyday Life in Bible Times ❧

For Sale: Roomy Tent, 2BR, No Leaks

The Hebrew patriarchs lived in large tents that were probably very much like the tents that Arab nomadic sheepherders live in today. These tents are made of goat's-hair fabric, which keeps out the rain and the heat. There are three seven-foot-high tent poles in a row down the middle and two rows on the outside. This design creates two rooms, one for women and children and one for men and guests.

Everyday Life in Israel

For most people, life was hard. Men and women worked hard in the fields raising crops or animals, and whole families helped out during harvest or sheep shearing time. Houses were small and cramped, and many people slept in the same room. Beds were usually straw mats on the floor. The women also worked hard preparing and cooking food and managing their households.

Cave Dwellings

There are many caves in Palestine, and early in history people lived in them. But the Old Testament does not mention anyone living in caves except in emergencies. Lot and his two daughters lived in a cave after Sodom and Gomorrah were destroyed. David and Elijah both hid in caves when their lives were in danger. The prophet Obadiah hid 100 prophets of the Lord from the wicked queen Jezebel in two caves.

Caves at Beit Guvrin, Israel

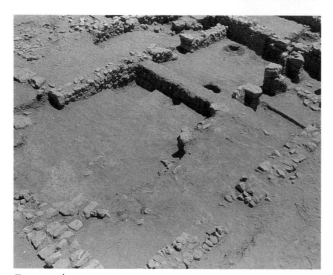

Four-room house

The Israelite Four-Room House

During the time of the monarchy in Israel, the most common type of house had four rooms. One room was long, running along the back wall. The other three rooms were side-by-side, next to the long room. People would enter the house through the middle room. Usually this room was used as a courtyard. This was a typically Israelite design, distinguishing Israelite settlements from Canaanite ones.

Children's Games

Bone flute

Many children's toys have been found in Israelite towns. These include whistles, rattles, marbles, dolls, and toy animals. Israelite children also kept pets, such as birds. Children danced, sang, and played games in the streets when they were not working. In 2 Kings 2, a band of small boys amused themselves by making fun of Elisha the prophet.

Building Materials

Almost all Israelite houses during Old Testament times were made of mud bricks. Sometimes rough stones were used along with the mud bricks. The walls were coated with waterproof plaster on the inside. The floors were made of hard-packed clay. Wealthier homes had floors paved with smooth stones. The roofs were made from wooden beams covered with branches, which were then filled in with mud plaster to make a flat surface.

"Adam and Eve Expelled From Paradise" by Mariotto Albertinelli

The World's First Clothes

Before Adam and Eve sinned, they did not wear any clothes and they were not embarrassed. But after they sinned, they were ashamed and made clothes for themselves. Their first clothes were not very substantial, however. They made aprons for themselves out of fig leaves. Later, God made them better clothes out of animal skins, which symbolized the animal sacrifices that would have to be offered for sin.

Making bricks

"Luke" by James J. Tissot

Medical Doctors in the Bible

Joseph used doctors to embalm his father, Jacob, in Egypt (Genesis 50:2). In Israel itself, King Asa of Judah sought medical help from doctors when he was sick (2 Chronicles 16:12). Usually God was the one who healed people in Old Testament times. Luke, the author of the books of Luke and Acts, was a doctor. In the New Testament period, medical science had advanced remarkably.

Joseph's Dream

Worry About Crops and Harvest

Life in Bible times was tightly bound up with the cycle of the seasons and the availability of food. Most of the Canaanite high gods were associated with the natural forces that brought rain and sunshine, since people lived only one bad year away from starvation. Joseph made a name for himself when he warned the pharaoh about an impending seven-year famine. Joseph organized food storage and distribution programs to combat it (Genesis 41).

Nurses in Israel

The midwife was the Israelite equivalent of a visiting nurse or public health worker. The Hebrews had professional midwives when they lived in Egypt who refused to obey the pharaoh's orders to kill Hebrew baby boys (Exodus 1). A midwife also helped Tamar when she had trouble giving birth to twins (Genesis 38).

Farmers' village

Farming Villages

Farmers in Palestine lived in small, crowded villages not far from their fields. Usually these villages were clustered together within a few miles of a walled city. That way, people in the villages could be under the protection of the fortified city if attackers came, but they were still close enough to their fields to work them.

Crop Planting

Israelite farmers plowed their fields with a simple hand plow made of wood, with a cone-shaped metal tip. This tip fitted over a wooden tailpiece that went into the ground. Plows were usually pulled by a team of oxen. The farmers planted seeds by scattering them on the fields by hand.

Gezer calendar

Planting and Harvesting Seasons

A very important calendar for the crop year was found in the biblical city of Gezer. This crop year begins in mid-September. It mentions two months of the olive harvest, two months of planting grain, two months of late planting, a month of hoeing flax, a month of barley harvest, another month of harvesting the other crops, two months of grape harvesting, and a month of summer fruit harvest.

"The Feast" by Sandro Botticelli

Solomon: No Vegetarian He

Meat was expensive food, served to guests only on very special occasions. Meat was common in royal palaces, however, because kings could afford it. The normal meat ration for one day in King Solomon's court was 10 oxen, 20 beef cows, 100 sheep, along with deer, gazelles, roebucks, and game birds (1 Kings 4:23)!

Dove's Dung

The Revised Standard Version in 2 Kings 6:25 mentions "dove's dung" selling for a good price during a siege of Samaria. Other versions have "locust beans" (New English Bible) or "wild onions" (New American Bible). It was a bulb that was roasted or boiled before eating. Today, the plant is known as the star of Bethlehem.

Fruits and Vegetables

Figs, dates, and pomegranates were the most common fruits eaten in Israel, after grapes, and they are mentioned frequently in the Bible. Apples, pears, apricots, quince, peaches, and melons are also known from the ancient Near East. Vegetables mentioned in the Bible include rice, lentils, beans, leeks, garlic, onions, and cucumbers.

Melons

The Israelites ate luscious watermelons and muskmelons when they were slaves in Egypt. These have been cultivated there since earliest times and were an inexpensive food for the captive Israelites. When they were in the parched wilderness, they longed for these juicy fruits and complained bitterly about their lack.

Spicy Foods

The Israelites spiced up their food with leeks, onions, and garlic when they lived in Egypt. They sorely missed these when they were eating nothing but manna and quail in the desert wilderness. Even today, many Israeli and Arab foods are flavored with exquisite spices.

Honey

The product of honeybees was a valued luxury during much of the Old Testament period, although in the New Testament wild honey was food for outcast John the Baptist (Matthew 3:4). Most honey was wild, but people brought honey from domesticated bees on at least one occasion to the Temple, among the other first fruits of the harvest (2 Chronicles 31:5).

Salt formations on the Dead Sea

"Salt that has lost its flavor"

This expression comes from Jesus, who compared his disciples to salt and their uselessness if they lost their "flavor," their commitment to Christ (Mark 9:50). Strictly speaking, sodium chloride (salt) is a stable compound and does not lose its saltiness. However, most salt in Palestine came from the Dead Sea, where other minerals and sand were mixed with it. The salt could dissolve, leaving a useless, tasteless compound.

Mint, Dill, and Cumin

These were green herbs mentioned by Jesus in his condemnation of many Pharisees' hypocrisy (Matthew 23:23). He said that they scrupulously gave a tenth of their supply of these herbs to God, in legalistic observance of the law, but that they neglected the more important things, such as justice, mercy, and faithfulness.

Manna

The Israelites were provided with "bread from heaven" in the wilderness. It appeared each morning as a fine, white, flaky substance on the ground that tasted like wafers and honey. Its name (Hebrew *man*) came from the puzzled Israelites, who asked "*man-hu?*" ("What is it?"). Certain insects in the Sinai Desert produce similar droppings, but not in such great quantities nor as often as told of in the Bible.

Insect droppings on a branch—Manna?

210

Olive orchard

Olive Farming

Olives grow on trees that are grown in orchards. These short, twisted trees do not need much attention until harvest time. In biblical times, olives were usually picked by hand, but sometimes they couldn't be reached so the farmers had to shake them off gently or beat the branches with long twigs or sticks. The olives then were crushed and pressed so the oil could be collected.

Oil lamp

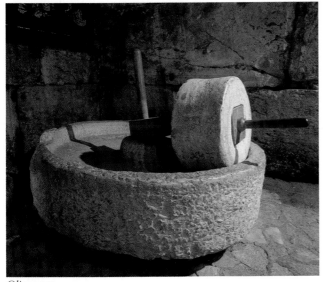

Olive press

Olive Oil

Along with bread and grapes, olive oil was the third most basic food. It was mixed with flour to make bread and cakes, and these were often cooked in the oil. It was also used as a fuel for lamps, in religious ceremonies, and as a medicinal ointment.

Oil Lamps

Oil lamps were the common means of lighting in biblical homes. They were made of clay or iron, and they burned olive oil for fuel. Thousands of oil lamps have been found, from all periods. Early lamps were flat bowls, and then a spout began to evolve with a pinched edge at the rim. Later lamps had a hole for the wick.

A Cubit

The cubit was the distance from the elbow to the tip of the middle finger of a grown man. It was the standard measure of length among the Hebrews. The standard cubit was approximately 17½ inches long, while the royal cubit was longer, about 20½ inches. God told Noah to build the ark 300 cubits long and 50 cubits wide.

Silver shekels

A Shekel for Your Thoughts

The shekel was the basic unit of weight in the ancient Near East. It was small, about four-tenths of an ounce. Small shekel weights in various denominations were used to weigh things on scales. The shekel is the basic coin in Israel today.

"Noah Building the Ark" from the Bedford Book of Hours

What's a Talent?

The talents in Jesus' parable of the master who gave his servants several talents were units of money. These were enormous sums of money, since the Greek *talanton* weighed between 57 and 95 pounds, and one talent was more than 15 years wages for a laborer. The modern English meaning of talent as ability was derived by expanding the meaning of the Greek word in this parable.

Roman baths at Hammath Gader

Ancient Baths

Washing and bathing were done in all biblical periods for religious and health reasons. Large public baths were introduced by the Greeks and Romans, and many remains of these have been found. Jesus healed a man by the Bethesda Pool, in the northeast corner of Jerusalem. This pool supposedly had healing properties.

Solomon's Bath

No, we aren't talking about how clean he was. The Hebrew *bath* was a unit of liquid measure, equal to almost six gallons (the royal bath was twice that). But the Hebrew word is not related to the English word. The large bronze "sea" in front of Solomon's Temple had a capacity of 2,000 baths.

Solomon

Stoning

Stoning was a form of ritual execution for certain prescribed crimes. These crimes included sacrificing a child to the god Molech, practicing witchcraft, blaspheming God's holy name, and leading people astray to worship other gods. Stoning was also a product of mob violence: Paul was stoned and left for dead at Lystra (Acts 14:19).

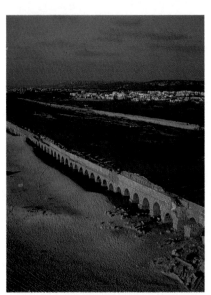

Roman aqueduct at Caesarea

Durable Roman Aqueducts

The Romans constructed magnificent aqueduct systems for cities throughout their empire. Jerusalem's aqueducts brought water into the city from as far away as 25 miles. These aqueducts were refurbished and used in many later periods, including under the British Mandate in 1918.

"Crucifixion" by Duccio

Crucifixion: Cruel and Unusual Punishment

Execution by crucifixion was normally reserved for the lower classes in Greek and Roman societies, usually slaves. It was a humiliating and excruciatingly slow, painful death. Prisoners were normally whipped until blood flowed, then they were either tied or nailed to the cross and left to die of gradual suffocation brought about by fatigue.

Pyramids of Giza, Egypt

Death

Death was the focus of much attention in almost every ancient Near Eastern society, where elaborate rituals and cults of the dead grew. The most elaborate systems arose in Egypt, where the pyramids and the great tombs of the kings were built to provide the pharaohs with everything necessary for the life to come. The Bible speaks of spiritual death as eternal separation from God.

Judas hangs himself.

Hanging

Hanging in the Old Testament meant the public exposure of a body after death. This was done as a warning to others, but a body was not exposed overnight (Deuteronomy 21:22,23). Two suicides were apparently by hanging: Ahithophel's (2 Samuel 17:23) and Judas Iscariot's (Matthew 27:5).

Dial-A-Mourner?

The prophet Jeremiah speaks of professional women mourners who could be summoned and who would "start a wailing for us." This skill was passed on to their daughters and even their neighbors (Jeremiah 9:17–20). But the Bible forbade any excessive displays of mourning for the dead: "You shall not cut yourselves or make any baldness on your foreheads for the dead" (Deuteronomy 14:1). These self-destructive customs were practiced by Israel's neighbors.

Roman age tomb

Impalement

The gruesome practice of impaling prisoners of war and criminals on stakes was practiced in several ancient societies. The Assyrians did this to prisoners of war, and the Persians did this as a criminal punishment, according to the Greek historian Herodotus. Haman's gallows in Esther was possibly a stake on which a person was impaled, rather than a hanging gallows.

Grave Robbers Beware!

In 1878, a Greek inscription labeled as an "Ordinance of Caesar" was brought to Europe, probably from Nazareth. Many scholars date it to about A.D. 50. It was 20 lines long and it proclaimed capital punishment for anyone who violated a grave in any way. This was an unusual feature of Roman law at this time.

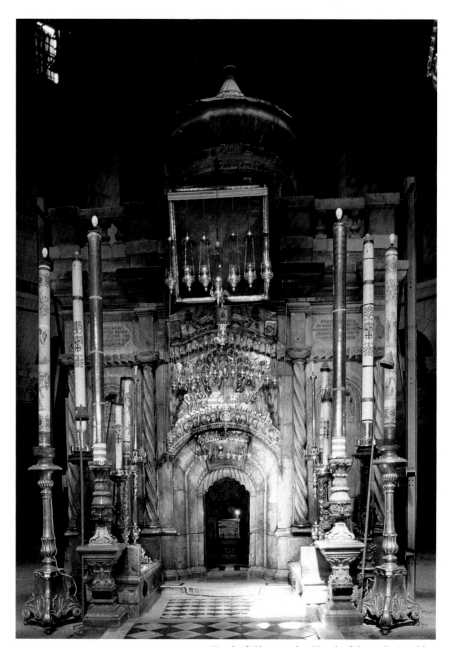

Tomb of Christ at the Church of the Holy Sepulchre

Jesus' Tomb and the Nazareth Decree

If the Ordinance of Caesar (also known as the Nazareth Decree) dates to A.D. 50, then the emperor Claudius issued it some 20 years after Jesus' death and resurrection. Some Jews said that Jesus' body was stolen from the grave (Matthew 28:11–15), so Claudius' decree may have been in reaction to this story. If so, it is the first extra-biblical indication that the Roman government was aware of Jesus.

Painting of those caring for Christ's body by Peiro della Francesca

Care for the Dead

Dead bodies were well cared for in all ancient societies. In the New Testament, we see examples of corpses being washed, anointed with aromatic preparations, and wrapped in linen cloths or bandages with a separate face cloth. Lack of burial was the ultimate humiliation. The evil queen Jezebel was left in the street and her flesh eaten by the dogs.

Ancient Cemeteries

Cemeteries have been some of the richest sources of information about life in the ancient world, because bodies were usually buried with important artifacts, and even food. Burials in Palestine were done in sealed caves, in large rock-cut chambers where many bodies were stored, and in burial boxes (ossuaries). The bones of infants were often buried in clay jars.

Jewish cemetery on Mount of Olives

"Creation of Eve" by Michelangelo

Eve: Mother of Life

Eve's name in Hebrew means "life" *(chavvah)*. Adam called his wife "Eve, because she was the mother of all living" (Genesis 3:20). The word for "living" (Hebrew *chayyah*) is related to Eve's name.

Adam: Earth Creature?

Adam's name (Hebrew *Adam*) is related to the word for earth or ground (Hebrew *adamah*). Undoubtedly this involves a play on words, since Adam was formed from "dust from the ground" (Genesis 2:7). Some modern works translate *Adam* as "earth creature" or "earthling" to emphasize this fact.

Adam

Gideon: Saint or Sinner?

Gideon was one of the Bible's heroes: God gave him a great victory over the Midianites (Judges 7). He then properly refused an offer to make him king as a result. However, he was not perfect. He made an ephod (a priestly garment of some sort—the high priest wore one) and Israel committed idolatry by worshiping with it. Judges 8:27 states that "it became a snare to Gideon and to his family."

Shamgar and Samson: Philistines' Nemeses

Samson was responsible for the death of several thousand Philistines (Judges 14–16). This was helpful to the Israelites, since the Philistines were their major antagonists. Once, he even killed 1,000 men with the jawbone of a donkey. Shamgar was a lesser-known judge, but he too killed many Philistines: 600 of them with an oxgoad (Judges 3:31).

Ecclesiasticus, Judith, and Gideon

"Samson Kills a Thousand Men" by James J. Tissot

"Naomi Entreating Ruth and Orpah to Return to the Land of Moab" by William Blake

Bittersweet Naomi

Naomi, Ruth's mother-in-law, lost her husband and her two sons. Her name means "pleasant," but she told people to call her *Mara*, which means "bitter" (Ruth 1:20). Fortunately, in the end, things were pleasant for Ruth and Naomi.

King Mesha, a Strange but Effective Tactician

Mesha, king of Moab, was an enemy of Israel's kings Ahab and Jehoram (2 Kings 3). He paid tribute to Ahab because Ahab was very powerful, but rebelled against Jehoram. When the battle went against him, Mesha sacrificed his oldest son on the wall of the city, in full view of the Israelites, which caused Israel to withdraw.

Mountains of Moab

Short People

Ahilud and his contemporaries during the biblical period of the judges (about the eleventh century B.C.) were short. Supporting pillars for roof beams in Ahilud's house at Raddana were only five feet three inches tall, and a beam hole in the house wall was also at the same height.

Ahilud's House

Ahilud was a homeowner in Raddana, near biblical Ai, during the days of Samuel. His house (his name was found inscribed on a jar handle) has been excavated. It was a modest house, with just two long, narrow rooms: one room was 6 feet by 40 feet and the other was 15 feet by 40 feet. Cooking was done outdoors and no bathrooms existed.

Ruins of Ai

Delilah: Samson's Lover

Delilah has become famous as a symbol of a treacherous seductress, since she was Samson's lover and the one who betrayed him to the Philistines. She did this by coaxing from him the secret to his great strength, which was his long hair (Judges 16). Contrary to popular thought, she did not cut his hair, but rather held his head on her lap (he was asleep) while the man she called in cut it.

"Samson and Delilah" by James J. Tissot

Unfortunate Agag

Agag was king of the Amalekites whom Saul captured alive and spared (1 Samuel 15). God's instructions had been to kill all the Amalekites, even the king. Samuel summoned the prisoner Agag, who came cheerfully because he thought and even said, "Surely the bitterness of death is past." Samuel, however, confronted him with his atrocities and then cut him up into many pieces.

The Ark of the Covenant

Ichabod: Born Under a Bad Sign

Samuel's daughter-in-law gave birth to a son at a bad time in Israel's history, just after the Ark of the Covenant—which represented God's presence and glory—had been captured by the Philistines. Because of this, she named her son *Ichabod*, which means "there is no glory" (or "where is the glory?").

Saul battles the Amalekites.

Saul and the Medium at Endor

Early in his reign, King Saul had tried to rid the land of the mediums and wizards. However, late in life, when God no longer answered his inquiries, he used the services of a medium to inquire about his upcoming battle with the Philistines. The medium called up Samuel from the dead, who was disturbed at being called, but who prophesied Saul's death.

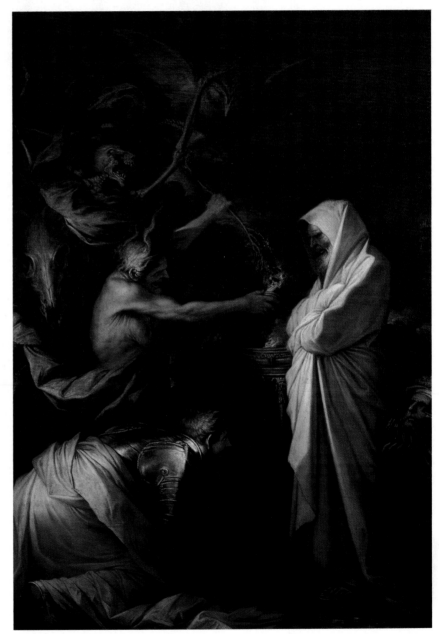

"Saul and the Witch of Endor" by Rosa Salvator

Jonathan: A Bighearted Man

Jonathan, Saul's son, won an impressive victory over the Philistines at the Pass of Michmash (1 Samuel 14), and he rightfully aspired to succeed his father as king. However, when it became clear that God had rejected his father's claim to the throne and that David would become king, he held no grudge and enthusiastically supported David.

241

David and Goliath: Test of Champions

When David met Goliath in a one-on-one confrontation, they were engaging in a relatively uncommon "contest of champions." Each army would pick its best warrior to do battle. The winning side was determined by the results of this contest, thereby avoiding much bloodshed and death. However, when David killed Goliath, the Israelites pursued and killed many Philistines, despite the ground rules.

"The Triumph of David" by Nicolas Poussin

Goliath's Spear

Goliath's spear is described as being "like a weaver's beam." This meant that it had a leash of cord wrapped around the spear shaft, with a loop into which he inserted his fingers. This was similar to a weaver's beam, which was a block of wood attached to a cord for separating the threads. This styling would have given the spear a spin, and thus a longer and truer trajectory.

"The Defiance of Goliath" by James J. Tissot

Og's Bed: Top-of-the-Line Model

Og, king of Bashan (an area northeast of the Jordan River), opposed the Israelites when they wanted to pass through his land of Bashan (Deuteronomy 3). He was a giant of a man. His bed was made of iron, and it was on display in Rabbah, capital of the Ammonites, for many years. It was more than 13 feet long and 6 feet wide!

Ishbosheth: Man of Shame

2 Samuel 2 calls Saul's son *Ishbosheth*, which means "man of shame." 1 Chronicles 8:33 gives his name as *Eshbaal*, which means "man of Baal." He was probably born as Eshbaal. However, the author of 2 Samuel substituted the name meaning "man of shame," rather than honor a pagan god by using the other name.

David's Kindnesses to Mephibosheth

David and Jonathan, one of Saul's sons, made a pact that they would remain loyal to each other and each other's posterity (1 Samuel 20). After Jonathan died, David inquired about his relatives. Mephibosheth, who was crippled, was the only one left, so David took him in like a son (2 Samuel 9).

"The Death of Absalom" by Francesco Pesellino

Absalom: Too Bigheaded for His Own Good

When Absalom—who had revolted against his father, David—was fleeing from some of his father's men, his head got caught in the thick branches of a large oak tree (2 Samuel 18:9). He was stuck fast enough that his servants discovered him hanging there, had a conversation about him, and then one of them decided to kill him, which he did.

"The Friendship of Jonathan and David" by James J. Tissot

Rebellious Sons

Several important characters in the Bible had sons who turned out badly. The two sons of Aaron, the high priest, offered unsanctioned sacrifices (Leviticus 10). The two sons of Eli the priest abused their priestly position and were called "worthless men" (1 Samuel 2). Samuel's two sons took bribes and perverted justice (1 Samuel 8).

Aaron

Ezekiel

Who Was Danel?

The New English Bible reads "Noah, Danel, and Job" in Ezekiel 14:14. This reflects the judgment that the "Daniel" in the Hebrew text was not Ezekiel's contemporary, but a semi-legendary Phoenician king named Danel, known from the Canaanite "Legend of Aqhat." In this way, the three figures would all have been ancient heroes. However, Ezekiel's point about righteousness according to the biblical God's standards would have been diluted had he used such an extra-biblical figure.

Did Huldah Go to College?

The King James Version states that the prophetess Huldah lived "in Jerusalem in the college" (2 Kings 22:14). This results from a misunderstanding of the Hebrew term *mishneh* (literally, "second"), which most modern versions translate as "Second Quarter" or "Second District." This area of Jerusalem was on the hill west of the Temple Mount.

Sanballat: Governor of Samaria

Sanballat was the leader of local opposition to Nehemiah's efforts in rebuilding the walls of Jerusalem (Nehemiah 4). An important extra-biblical document found among the Elephantine Papyri on the Nile, dating shortly after the Book of Nehemiah, mentions Sanballat and his sons: "Delaiah and Shelemiah, the sons of Sanballat the governor of Samaria."

Nehemiah's wall

Jerusalem

250

"Ahab Pierced by an Arrow" by James J. Tissot

Micaiah: Principled Prophet

When kings Ahab and Jehoshaphat wanted to go out to war, they consulted 400 of Ahab's prophets, who told them that God would be with them. Jehoshaphat wanted a second opinion, so they sent for Micaiah. Ahab hated Micaiah, because "he never prophesies good concerning me, but evil" (1 Kings 22:8). True to form, Micaiah formed a minority of one in speaking against Ahab, but his was a true prophecy from God.

Micaiah's Humor

Ahab's 400 false prophets told him to "Go up into battle; for the Lord will give the enemy into your hand" (1 Kings 22:6). Micaiah's first response to Ahab's inquiry was exactly the same, word for word. However, Ahab recognized Micaiah's sarcastic humor, and urged him to tell the truth, which he then did: Micaiah had a message of doom for Ahab.

Figs

Amos: Not a Prophet Nor a Son of a Prophet

When the prophet Amos protested that he was not a prophet nor a prophet's son (Amos 7:14), he meant that he had not been raised or trained as a prophet, and he did not make his living prophesying. He did not live with other prophets in one of the prophetic schools. Rather, he had his own profession—he was a herdsman and a dresser of sycamore figs—and he was prophesying only because God had sent him on a special mission.

Malachi: God's Messenger

The Hebrew word *malachi* means "my messenger" and it is also the name of the prophet Malachi. The word is found twice in the Book of Malachi, where it refers once to each, in an obvious play on words.

Ezekiel

Ezekiel: Widowed Prophet

Ezekiel's wife, the "delight of his eyes," was taken from him by God, but Ezekiel was instructed not to mourn, weep, or make any public display for her. This was to foreshadow God's destroying the Temple, the "delight of Judah's eyes," which Judah was not to mourn, since Judah had so greatly profaned it and its worship.

Malachi   256

Who Were the Hasidic Jews?

The Hebrew term *hasidim* means "pious ones," and it is often translated in the Bible as "saints." An identifiable group of Jews called the Hasideans arose during the period between the Old and New Testaments. They resisted the politicalization of the office of high priest during this period, and also the movement toward political independence. Most scholars think the Hasideans were the precursors to the Pharisees.

Abraham and Melchizedek

Melchizedek: King and Priest

Melchizedek was a shadowy figure known mainly from one story in Genesis 14. He was king of Salem (Jerusalem) and "a priest of God Most High." He pronounced a blessing on Abraham, and Abraham gave him a tithe of all he had. A tithe is a tenth, which, under the Law that came later, was to be given to the priests and Levites.

Modern Hasidism

Modern Hasidism is a religious and social movement that began in the eighteenth century in Eastern Europe. It represented a rebellion against the elite scholarship that had developed in Judaism. Hasidism taught that all could know God equally well, and it emphasized experiential religion, including joyful celebration of life, earnest devotion to God, and even ecstatic experiences. *The Chosen*, a novel made into a movie, sensitively portrays life in a modern Hasidic community.

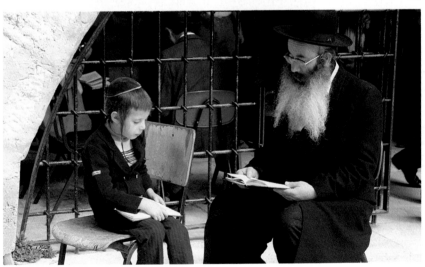

Peter the Rock

Peter's name in Greek *(Petros)* means "rock" *(petra)*. A climactic point in Jesus' ministry came when Peter confessed that Jesus was the Messiah, the Son of God. Jesus blessed him and said, "You are Peter *[Petros]*, and on this rock *[petra]* I will build my church" (Matthew 16:18).

"Jesus Gives Keys to St. Peter" by Vincenzo de Biagio

The Bible's Two Sauls

Both men named Saul in the Bible were scoundrels. Saul, the first king of Israel, disqualified himself from being king by his disobedient actions, and he had mental disturbances that caused him to try to kill David several times. Saul of Tarsus was a Jew who persecuted the early Christians. However, he was converted and became the great Apostle Paul!

Peter crucified upside down.

Peter: Crucified Upside Down?

Christian tradition states that when the Apostle Peter was martyred, he asked to be crucified upside down, since he was not worthy to be crucified in the same manner as his Lord was. This may not have been an unusual mode of crucifixion. Some evidence suggests that condemned criminals may have had their heels nailed together and their legs hung over the top of the cross.

"Conversion of St. Paul" by Caravaggio

"School of Athens" by Raphael

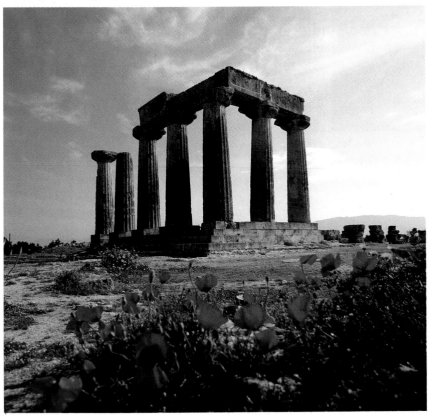

Temple of Apollo at Corinth

Stoics: Pursuers of Virtue

Acts 17:18 mentions Stoic philosophers who argued with Paul at Athens, where they challenged his view of the resurrection of the dead. Paul even quoted a Stoic poet, Aratus, in his argument (verse 28). Stoic philosophy concentrated upon logic, physics, and ethics. Their ethical striving for virtue is their best-known emphasis, in contrast to the Epicureans, who strove to avoid pain.

Priscilla and Aquila: A Good Team

Priscilla and Aquila were Jews from Corinth who were coworkers with Paul. They instructed Apollos, a gifted teacher, in the ways of Jesus, and they provided hospitality for Paul in their home (Acts 18). Priscilla is usually mentioned first, suggesting to some scholars that she played the leading role in the couple's ministry.

Tent-Makers Today

The term "tent-maker" is often used today to describe someone who supports his or her Christian ministry by practicing a trade on the side, as Paul did. Paul argued in 1 Corinthians 9 that Christian workers had every right to be paid by those to whom they ministered, but he personally refrained from claiming this right, so as not to put even the slightest obstacle in the way of his ministry.

Barabbas: Freed Prisoner

Barabbas is known only as the criminal Pilate released instead of Jesus. He is described in the Gospels as "a notorious prisoner" (Matthew 27:16), one of "the rebels in prison, who had committed murder in the insurrection" (Mark 15:7), and "a robber" (John 18:40). Pilate used a custom of releasing a prisoner at Passover (which is not otherwise known), and offered the people a choice: Jesus or Barabbas. The people chose Barabbas.

"Christ Interrogated by Pilate" by Duccio

Joseph of Arimathea: Caretaker of Jesus' Body

Joseph of Arimathea (a village in Judea) was a wealthy member of the Sanhedrin who came forward and offered his own tomb for Jesus' burial (Luke 23:50–56). He was given Jesus' body and, with help from Nicodemus, wrapped the body and buried it. Later outrageous legends state that Joseph was sent to England by the Apostle Paul, that he took the Holy Grail there, and that he freed Ireland from snakes.

"Joseph of Arimathea" by James J. Tissot

"George Washington they're not!"

In popular American mythology, George Washington confessed to chopping down a cherry tree by saying, "I cannot tell a lie." Ananias and Sapphira were husband and wife who sold some land and donated part of the money to the church. However, they lied about it, claiming their donation was the entire amount. For this, they were both struck dead on the spot (Acts 5).

Caesar Augustus on coin

Caesar, Kaiser Wilhelm, and the Russian Czars

Caesar was the family name of the Julian family of Rome, whose most famous member was the emperor Caius Julius Caesar (102 to 44 B.C.). This family name was passed down to all Roman emperors until Hadrian (A.D. 117 to 138). The German word *kaiser* and the Russian word *czar* both come from Caesar.

Roman gold coins

"The Stoning of St. Stephen" by Adam Elsheimer

"Render unto Caesar"

Some Pharisees tried to trap Jesus by asking him whether they should pay taxes to Caesar. If he said yes, they could accuse him of neglecting God's way. If he said no, he could be accused of subversion of Roman law. Jesus frustrated them by simply showing them a coin with Caesar's likeness on it and stating, "Render to Caesar the things that are Caesar's, and to God the things that are God's" (Mark 12:17).

Stephen: The First Christian Martyr

Stephen was a deacon, he performed many miracles, and he spoke wise words from God. This displeased many Jewish leaders and trumped-up charges were brought against him. He delivered a long indictment of these leaders, accusing them of complicity in Jesus' death. This enraged them so much that they interrupted his speech, dragged him out of the city, and stoned him to death (Acts 6–8).

Simon and "Simony"

The English word "simony" refers to the practice of buying or selling ecclesiastical pardons or offices. It comes from Simon the Magician, who, after his conversion, tried to buy spiritual power from the Apostles after he saw them laying hands on people and the people receiving the Holy Spirit (Acts 8).

Gazelles

Beloved Tabitha, the Seamstress

Tabitha, a disciple of Jesus, died in the city of Joppa when Peter was in a neighboring town. Tabitha was beloved in the community, as she "was full of good works and acts of charity" (Acts 9:36). The widows especially missed her, and they showed Peter many of the garments she had made for them. Peter prayed for her and she was made alive again. Her Greek name was Dorcas; both of her names mean "gazelle."

Holy Spirit

A Real Sleepyhead

Eutychus, a young man from Troas, fell asleep one evening while he was listening to a sermon by Paul that lasted well past midnight. Unfortunately, he was sitting in a window on the second floor, and he toppled out and died. Fortunately, however, Paul brought him back to life (Acts 20).

"The Crucifixion" by G. Battista and G. Tiepolo

The First *Christians*

A Christian was a follower of Jesus the Christ (Jesus the Messiah). As the Church grew, the followers of Christ became more noticeable, but it wasn't until several years after Jesus died that the disciples were first called Christians. This happened at Antioch of Syria (Acts 11:26).

What Was an Apostle?

The Greek word *apostolos* ("apostle") comes from *apostello*, which means "to send." In secular Greek usage, *apostolos* often meant "ship," "fleet," or "naval expedition" (something sent out), but almost never did it mean a person sent. In the New Testament, the meaning was attached to people appointed (or sent) to special functions in the church. Usually it referred to the 12 Disciples of Jesus or to Paul.

The Sumerians

The Sumerians flourished in southern Mesopotamia in the third millennium B.C. They are credited with the invention of writing about 3200 B.C., and they produced a long list of literary, historical, and mythological-religious works. They also developed advanced systems of laws, mathematics, and astronomy.

The Egyptians

Egyptian civilization flourished in relative isolation in the long, narrow Nile Valley for almost 3,000 years, until it was overrun by Persians and then Greeks. Its golden age came in the second half of the second millennium B.C., which included the time when Moses lived there. Egyptians built great temples and pyramids, developed a complex writing system and a great literature, and had a complex religious system emphasizing gods of the dead.

"The Last Supper" by Ghirlandaio

Egyptian temple at Abu Simbel

❧ GEOGRAPHY ❧

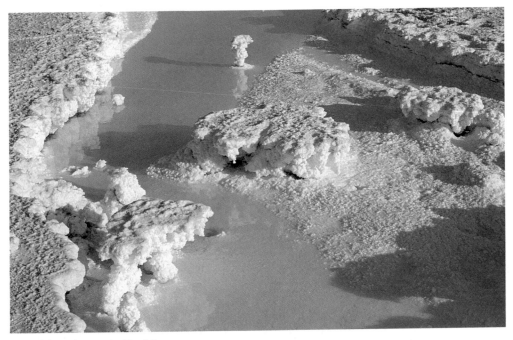

Mineral formations on the Dead Sea

The Lowest Place on Earth

The lowest point on the face of the earth is the surface of the
Dead Sea. It is about 1,300 feet below sea level. The Dead Sea
is part of the Great Rift Valley that runs north and south
through eastern Africa. This valley includes the Jordan Valley
to the north of the Dead Sea and parts of the Red Sea to
the south.

A Truly "Dead" Sea

Because of its high concentrations of salt and other minerals,
no fish can live in the Dead Sea. That is how it got its name.
It is nestled in a hostile, barren valley with very few plants
surrounding it, but there is an oasis or two. Its southern
shoreline is dotted with strange geological formations that
make it look like a moonscape.

Dead Sea

279

The Cilician Gates

The Apostle Paul traveled throughout Asia Minor (modern Turkey), and he would have seen some spectacular scenery along the way. Near his hometown of Tarsus in southeastern Asia Minor was the Taurus mountain range, which completely blocked off east-west travel. The one route through these mountains was through the Cilician Gates, a deep, narrow pass through wild, rugged terrain.

Roman milestones

One More Milestone for Israel

The Romans used distinctive milestones to mark distances on their roads. These were small, round stone columns set on bases by the sides of the roads. The Romans were master engineers, building extensive networks of good roads throughout their empire, along which the Apostle Paul and others traveled. The roads were built using large slabs of stone. Many of these, including the milestones, are still on Israel's roads today.

Cilician Gates

Looking for Noah in All the Wrong Places?

Many modern-day expeditions have searched for Noah's ark on the snow- and glacier-covered slopes of Mount Ararat, a 17,000-foot peak in Armenia, in eastern Turkey. However, the Bible says that the ark came to rest on "the mountains of Ararat" (Genesis 8:4), which may mean anywhere in mountainous Armenia.

Noah's Ark

Oasis of Jericho

What? No Sand Dunes?!

For the most part, deserts in Bible lands do not have the great shifting sand dunes that are found in many deserts. Most of these deserts are dry, flat, and rocky. The hot desert winds blow fine dust or sand across the barren surface. Occasionally oases with springs and palm trees can be found.

Mesopotamia and Hippopotami

Mesopotamia was the fertile region of land between the Tigris and Euphrates rivers, in present-day Iraq, and was the home of the ancient Sumerian, Babylonian, and Assyrian empires. Its name means "the land between *(meso)* the rivers *(potamoi)*." The word hippopotamus is related: It means "river *(potamos)* horse *(hippus)*."

Biblical Deserts

Palestine was bordered by two great deserts. The great Arabian Desert stretched out to the east and southeast and the Sinai Desert was to the south. Within Israel itself, the southern part was called the Negev Desert and the area east of Jerusalem was the wilderness of Judea. It was hilly, but it was dry and parched like a desert.

Negev Desert

Mount Gerizim

Life in the Desert

As is even true today, desert dwellers built their lives around raising sheep and goats, which provided dairy products and meat. These animals also provided materials for clothing and tents. A major concern in the desert was finding water, so many wells were dug and people found oases. Year-round streams or rivers were not common, but in the rainy season there were many.

Streams in the Desert

Oases were well known in biblical times. The Israelites stayed at the oasis of Kadesh-barnea, in the northern Sinai Desert. The famous site of En-Gedi, the location of a perennial spring in the Judean wilderness near the Dead Sea, is mentioned several times in the Bible. A beautiful waterfall cascades down several hundred feet from this spring, which is a popular resort center today.

The Navel of the Earth

Many ancient Near Eastern societies developed the concept of their cities or land being at the center of all things—the "navel" of the earth. In the Bible, two places—Shechem, near the religiously significant Mount Gerizim, and the land of Israel itself—are so called. Most English versions today translate the Hebrew phrase as middle (or center) of the earth.

En-Gedi

Jerusalem

Jerusalem: City of Shalo[m]

When the Israelites took over Je[rusalem, they were] offended by its many gods and [   ] they gave its name a new meani[ng   ] *(Shalom)*. This was possible beca[use   ] just like the Hebrew words for '[   ] title has remained a symbol of [   ] city ever since.

Kidron Valley

Mount Zion

Mount Zion: The Highest of All Hills

The term Mount Zion originally referred to the low hill of Jerusalem on which King David built his early city. Later, it was transferred to the higher hill to the west. It came to symbolize the capital of God's kingdom, and Isaiah and Micah spoke of Mount Zion as ultimately being established as "the highest of the mountains...raised above the hills."

Staying Close to Home

Jesus spent almost all of the first year and a half of his public ministry in the region of Galilee, where he grew up. Many important highways passed through Galilee, going to distant places. Thus, Jesus could have had easy contact with a wide variety of people without traveling very far and without exposing himself early in his ministry to the anger of the religious authorities in Jerusalem.

A Blast of Hot Air

The prophet Amos speaks of God roaring like a lion from Jerusalem because he is angry with the nation of Israel and the blast of his roar causing the top of Mount Carmel to wither. Mount Carmel is a lush, wooded mountain more than 70 miles north of Jerusalem. God's breath not only reaches Carmel, but it scorches the shepherd's pastures between these two points as well (Amos 1:2).

Mount Carmel

Galilee

A Hidden Water Tunnel

The Jebusites who lived in Jerusalem before King David were responsible for an ingenious tunnel system that brought fresh water into their city from the hidden spring in the valley below. They tunneled straight down through the hill above the spring and tapped into an underground stream. They would lower buckets and fill them from this stream and not have to go outside the protection of the city walls.

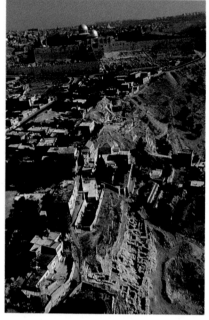

Ruins of David's City

The City of David

The city that David captured from the Jebusites and lived in was small, about 15 acres in size. It was a walled city built on a low, elongated hill, next to which was a hidden spring. It was a significant city despite its size, and David was able to use many of the existing buildings and even some of the existing bureaucracy in setting up his kingdom.

Heavenly Jerusalem— Bigger than a Rubik's Cube

In the Apostle John's vision of heavenly Jerusalem (Revelation 21 and 22), he saw a shimmering, bejewele[d] city descend from heaven. [The] city was a spectacular fantas[y] however, since it was a perf[ect] cube measuring 1,500 miles each side—the distance fro[m] New York City to Housto[n]. [It] had a miniature wall totally out of proportion to the ot[her] dimensions. It was clearly symbolic of the glories that [lie] ahead.

Jerusalem: An Out-of-the-Way Place

Jerusalem was not easy to get [to. It] was not located on either of t[he] major north-south trade or military routes, the coastal "V[ia] of the Sea," or the eastern "K[ing's] Highway" on the Plains of M[oab]. So even though tiny Israel wa[s] constantly being squeezed between the world's large em[pires] on either side of it and powe[rful] foreign armies frequently ma[rched] through it on their missions [of] conquest, Jerusalem remaine[d] relatively secure as Israel's ca[pital].

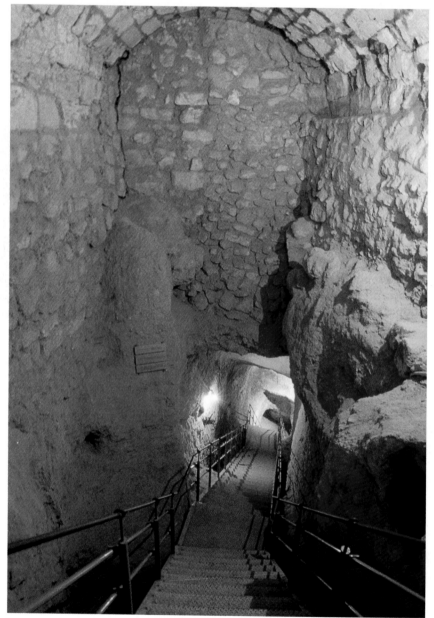

Water tunnel system (Warren's shaft) in Jerusalem

How David Captured Jerusalem

Jerusalem's water supply was its weak point, and David exploited it in capturing the city. He challenged his men to "strike at the water shaft," which they did, either by cutting off the water supply or by going up the tunnel itself into the city (2 Samuel 5:7–9).

Tourists at David's Tomb

Tourists in Jerusalem can see the Tomb of David on the south-western hill, which is today called Mount Zion. However, this tomb dates no earlier than the ninth century, some 1,800 years after David. His actual burial place is unknown.

Water Through a Rock

One of the great engineering feats recorded in the Bible was the 1,750-foot-long tunnel—through bedrock 150 feet under the City of David in Jerusalem—that was dug during King Hezekiah's reign. Its purpose was to direct water inside the city walls from a hidden spring, thus providing a reliable water source in time of siege. It was laboriously hacked out of the rock with pickaxes by two crews digging toward each other.

Tomb of King David

Hezekiah's Water Tunnel

Let's Meet in the Middle!

A 2,500-year-old inscription carved into stone was found in 1880 near the south end of Hezekiah's water tunnel. The inscription tells the proud story of the climactic labors of its construction crews. It tells of the stonecutters swinging their pickaxs, and then of the excitement of hearing the other workers: "the voice of a man calling to his fellow." They soon were able to meet: "The quarrymen hewed the rock, each man toward his fellow, ax against ax, and the water flowed from the spring toward the reservoir."

Chapel of the Ascension

Akeldama

Jesus' Footprints?

The Chapel of the Ascension on the Mount of Olives supposedly marks the spot where Jesus ascended to heaven. It was built during Crusader times (in the eleventh century) over a spot marked since the fourth century. A stone slab contains what some claim are Jesus' last footprints on earth.

Judas' Tainted Money

Deuteronomy 23:18 states that "You shall not bring the fee of a prostitute or the wages of a male prostitute into the house of the Lord...for...these are abhorrent to [him]." In accordance with this principle, the priests did not put Judas' 30 pieces of silver into the Temple treasuries, since it was "blood money." Instead, they purchased a field to bury strangers in, called potter's field.

Akeldama: Field of Blood

Akeldama was the Aramaic name, meaning "field of blood," given to the field bought with the 30 pieces of silver that Judas received when he betrayed Jesus. The name seems to be due to two reasons: the spilling of Judas' blood (Acts 1:18,19), and the fact that the field was bought with "blood money" (from Jesus' betrayal) (Matthew 27:6). Today, residents of Jerusalem still say they can identify the field.

Dome of the Rock

The Dome of the Rock

A magnificent golden-colored dome dominates the view of the Old City in Jerusalem today. It sits atop an eight-sided building built over the large rock that is significant in both Jewish and Muslim traditions. The first Muslim dome was built in the seventh century A.D., shortly after the Arab capture of Jerusalem in A.D. 638.

Islamic and Jewish Art: Close Cousins

The most distinctive feature of Islamic religious art is its abstract nature: No living creatures are represented. Exquisite examples of this are found on the walls of the Dome of the Rock, and on the underside of the great dome itself. This prohibition against representing living things is similar to (but stricter than) the Jewish prohibition against making any representations of God himself.

Abraham's Rock?

A large rock measuring 58 feet long by 51 feet wide by 4 to 6 feet high sits squarely in the middle of the Temple Mount. Different traditions say that this is the rock upon which Abraham offered his son Isaac as a sacrifice, where the great altar of Solomon's Temple stood, and from where Mohammed ascended to heaven. Today, the great Muslim Dome of the Rock stands over the spot.

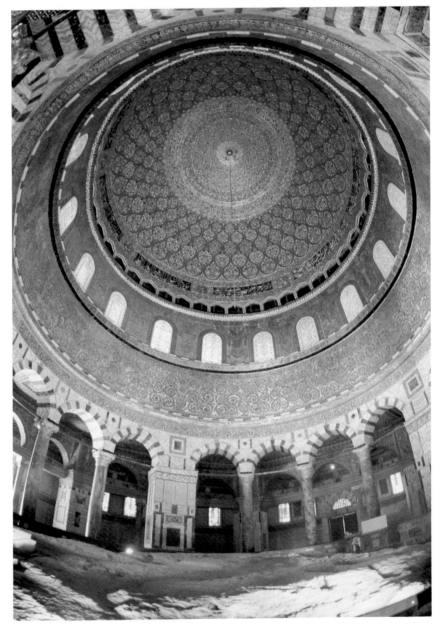

Interior of the Dome of the Rock

Close up of mosaic   293

❧ GEOGRAPHY ❧

Jerusalem: A Holy City for Three Faiths

Jerusalem is holy to Jews, Christians, and Muslims alike. For Jews, it was the site that David chose as his capital city and where the Temple was built. For Christians, it was where Jesus ministered, died, rose again, and ascended to heaven. For Muslims, it was the place from which the prophet Mohammed was transported to heaven.

Ebla: A Major Discovery

Ebla was the capital of an important Semitic kingdom in northern Syria during the third millennium B.C. Its significance was not realized until after 1975, when a major cache of thousands of documents was found there. Ebla was a large city, a major commercial center, and these texts have shed light on many aspects of ancient life in the earliest biblical times.

Jericho: The World's Oldest City

A fine spring waters Jericho, which was first occupied in 9000 B.C. It was an oasis in the Jordan Valley, and was called the City of the Palms in the Bible. The Israelites captured it under Joshua, in the famous incident when its walls collapsed. It lay as a sparsely-inhabited ruin for more than 1,000 years, when it was rebuilt by King Herod.

Muslims praying at the Dome of the Rock.

Walls of Jericho excavated.

Jericho

Ugarit: Great Canaanite City-State

Ugarit flourished on the northeastern Mediterranean coast in the fourteenth and thirteenth centuries B.C., close to the time that the Israelites entered the land of Canaan. Its discovery in 1929 revealed first-hand texts of Canaanite religion, including the worship of Baal. Many Ugaritic texts are poetic, in a language and style similar to that of the biblical psalms.

A Curse Fulfilled

Joshua's curse on Jericho stated that anyone rebuilding Jericho would pay a stiff price (Joshua 6:26): "At the cost of his first-born shall he lay its foundation, and at the cost of his youngest son shall he set up its gates." Many years later, a man named Hiel, from Bethel, did some rebuilding, but it cost him his oldest and youngest sons (1 Kings 16:34), in fulfillment of this prophecy. Today, there is an Arab town called Jericho, but it is not built on the biblical site.

Thebes: City of Temples and Tombs

The Egyptian city of Thebes flourished during the latter half of the second millennium B.C., when Moses and the Israelites were in Egypt. Several magnificent temples were built there, and the Valley of the Kings burial tombs were nearby. The Book of Nahum mentions Thebes' destruction in 663 B.C.

Thebes

295

Nineveh: Assyrian Capital

Nineveh, on the Tigris River, reached its height of glory as Assyria's capital under Sennacherib and Ashurbanipal. Sennacherib built a fabulous palace with more than 71 rooms, 10,000 feet of sculptured walls, and 27 gateways formed by huge winged bulls and sphinxes. Ashurbanipal's palace contained uncounted treasures of sculpture and art work, and a library with thousands of texts.

Prism of Sennacherib

Life of Alexander the Great

Alexandria: Greek Center of Learning

Alexandria was founded by Alexander the Great in 331 B.C. in the western Nile Delta in Egypt. It soon became a great intellectual, cultural, commercial, and scientific center for many centuries following. It housed a library of 480,000 volumes at one time. It was here that Greek-speaking Jews translated the Hebrew Bible into Greek, making it accessible to thousands of readers, including the writers of the New Testament.

Babylon: Destroyer of Jerusalem

Babylon had a long history, extending into the post biblical period. Its greatest glory came in the seventh and sixth centuries B.C., during which time it also captured Jerusalem. It had a 280-foot-high pyramid-shaped temple tower that may have been the biblical Tower of Babel, along with many other impressive temples. Thousands of religious and mythological texts have been recovered from Babylon, as well as extremely accurate historical records.

"The Tower of Babel" by Pieter Brueghel

Rome: Oppressor and Nurturer of Christianity

Rome was founded in 753 B.C., and it became the capital of one of the greatest empires of the ancient world. Its systems of government and communication allowed for the rapid spread of Christianity after Jesus' death. The Apostle Paul's great desire was to take the Gospel message to Rome, from which Christianity was to spread throughout the world. Rome was also a symbol of great evil in the New Testament.

Roman Forum

Corinth: The Las Vegas of the Roman Empire

Corinth was an important Greek city, located on the isthmus joining the Pelopponesian Peninsula to mainland Greece. It was an important commercial center, and the Apostle Paul chose to establish a church there because of its strategic importance. Corinth in Paul's time was an extremely decadent city, as his letters to the Corinthian church show.

Corinth

Jonah

Where Was Tarshish?

The Book of Jonah states that Jonah took a ship going to Tarshish rather than go to Nineveh, as God had commanded him. Tarshish was either part of the island of Sardinia (off the coast of Italy) or a region in far-off Spain. It is obvious that Jonah's intent was to go as far away from Nineveh as he could.

Fish Stories: Jonah and Nineveh

A delightfully ironic connection between Jonah and Nineveh can be seen through the fish imagery. Jonah found himself enclosed within the walls of a great fish's belly because he refused to go to Nineveh, which was known as the great fish city that was enclosed within its own walls.

Nineveh's Library

A vast library of more than 26,000 clay tablets was discovered at Nineveh in the 1850s in the palaces of Sennacherib and Ashurbanipal. This was the most important find for deciphering the languages of Assyria, and they have provided invaluable insight into its history and culture. The tablets were very carefully numbered and catalogued in series.

Petra: City in the Cliffs

The ancient city of Petra (probably biblical Sela) is a spectacular city of temples, tombs, buildings, and monuments carved deep into the rock cliffs of a long, narrow gorge in the desert east of the Dead Sea. It was settled by the Nabateans, a people who lived there beginning in the fourth century B.C., and it rose to become an important commercial center.

Jonah

Petra

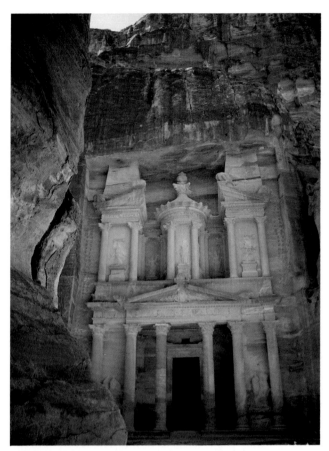

Petra

Petra's "Treasury of the Pharaoh"

The most magnificent monument at Petra is the *Khazneh Far`un*, the "Treasury of the Pharaoh." It is a great temple carved deep into the breathtaking reddish-pink sandstone, with impressive columns and other ornate carvings. Even Hollywood has discovered Petra! The third film of the Indiana Jones series was filmed there.

The Bible's Earthquakes

The Bible mentions three actual earthquakes. One was during the reign of Uzziah (Amos 1:1), another was on the day of Jesus' crucifixion just after he died (Matthew 27:51–53), and a third occurred when Paul and Silas were imprisoned at Philippi (Acts 16:26). This last earthquake broke open the doors of the prison so that prisoners could have escaped, causing the jailer great distress. Paul and Silas, however, reassured the jailer that everyone was still there.

Solar Eclipse

Solar and Lunar Eclipses

The Bible mentions eclipses several times, as prophetic signs of God's judgment. Amos 8:9 states that "I will make the sun go down at noon, and darken the earth in broad daylight." Joel 2:31 says that "The sun shall be turned to darkness, and the moon to blood." Lunar eclipses do indeed look red at times, due to refraction of the sun's light.

"The Death of Jesus" by James J. Tissot

299

Great Rift Valley

The Great Rift Valley

The Great Rift Valley that runs north and south in eastern Africa extends north into Bible lands. It forms the Jordan Valley basin, which includes the Sea of Galilee, the Jordan River, and the Dead Sea. It is the joining point for two great tectonic plates that slowly slide past each other. Zechariah 14:4 mentions the Mount of Olives being split in two "so that one half...shall withdraw northward, and the other half southward."

Rain and Drought

Life in Palestine depended heavily on rain, in contrast to Egypt and Mesopotamia, where great river systems provided water for crops. Without rain, drought set in and famine was just around the corner. The highest Canaanite god, Baal, was the god of the storms. People wanted to please him, since they thought he could send rain.

The *Khamsin*: Hot East Wind

A hot south and east wind blows across Egypt and Palestine during the months of May and October. It fills the air with a yellow haze of dust and often lasts three days or more. The Bible mentions this wind many times as a symbol of God's wrath. Isaiah 27:8 states that God removed his people into exile "with his fierce blast in the day of the east wind."

❧ GEOGRAPHY ❧

Pass of Michmash

The Pass of Michmash

Michmash was a town southeast of Bethel where Saul and Jonathan had an encounter with the Philistines (1 Samuel 13,14). The Philistines guarded the narrow pass, but Jonathan and his armor-bearer scaled the cliffs and launched a surprise attack. They killed 20 men and routed the Philistines.

The Cave of Machpelah

This was the cave that Abraham bought to bury his wife Sarah in, near Hebron (Genesis 23). Abraham, Isaac, and Jacob also were buried there. Abraham's purchase was significant, since it represented the first clear title to the land that God had promised him. A mosque marks the spot of this cave today.

Qumran cave

Biblical Caves

Caves were abundant in Palestine. They were used as dwelling places (Genesis 19:30), as hiding places (1 Samuel 22:1), and as burial places (John 11:38). The most common types of caves were formed by the action of underground water, where the water table eventually receded and left a cave. The dryness of many caves made them ideal for storage. The Dead Sea Scrolls survived almost two thousand years in caves, without much deterioration.

Machpelah

⚜GEOGRAPHY⚜

The Garden of Eden: A Biblical Paradise

The Garden of Eden was the lush paradise where God placed the first man and woman.

Genesis 2:8 speaks of Eden as a land in which the garden was placed, however: "And the Lord God planted a garden in Eden, in the east." Several passages speak of it as "the garden of the Lord."

Adam and Eve

The Seven Wonders of the Ancient World

The seven wonders of the ancient world come from the lists of Antipater of Sidon and Philon of Byzantium, travelers in the late pre-Christian era. The wonders are the Great Pyramid at Giza (Egypt), the Hanging Gardens of Babylon, the Statue of Zeus at Olympia (Greece), the Temple of Diana at Ephesus (Asia Minor), the Mausoleum (tomb) at Halicarnassus (Asia Minor), the Colossus of Rhodes (Aegean Sea), and the Pharos (Lighthouse) at Alexandria (Egypt).

The Great Pyramid at Giza

The Great Pyramid was built as a tomb for the Egyptian pharaoh Khufu at Giza, near modern-day Cairo (about 2700 B.C.). It contains nearly two and a half million stone blocks, each weighing at least two and a half metric tons. It covers an area of 13 acres, and originally rose 481 feet high. It is the only ancient wonder still surviving today. It had already stood for centuries when Joseph and Moses lived in Egypt.

The Hanging Gardens of Babylon

These gardens were built some time in the eighth to sixth centuries B.C. They did not actually hang, but were roof gardens laid out on a series of terraces and were irrigated by pumps, reaching about 350 feet high. The water trickled down over the terraces, but did not seep through, since the stone balconies were roofed with reeds, bitumen, and lead. The Jews exiled in Babylon would have been impressed by the sight of these.

Giza pyramids

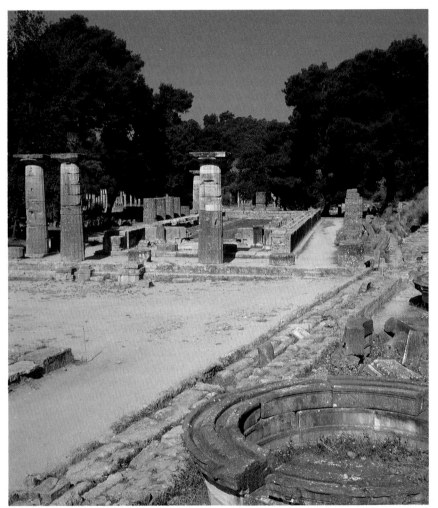

Temple of Hera in Olympia, Greece

Statue of Artemis from Ephesus

The Mausoleum at Halicarnassus

A brilliant white marble tomb, built by King Mausolus (hence mausoleum) for his wife Atremesia in the fourth century B.C., stood on a hill overlooking the Greek port of Halicarnassus. It stood 140 feet high and was covered by a pyramid dome. Sculptured horses and lions adorned its courtyards and roof. A colony of Jews lived at Halicarnassus in the second and first centuries B.C.

The Statue of Zeus at Olympia

A huge figure of Zeus, the Greek storm god and head of the pantheon, stood 40 feet high in a great temple of Zeus at Olympia, in Greece. It was sculpted about 456 B.C. out of wood, with thin plates of gold and ivory completely covering it. Its eyes were large jewels and its robes were covered with precious stones.

The Temple of Diana at Ephesus

Diana was the Roman name for the Greek goddess Artemis, whose principal shrine was a great temple at Ephesus, on the coast of Asia Minor. The Ephesian Artemis was the goddess of fertility. This magnificent temple was said by Philon to be the greatest of the seven wonders. It was built of white marble and overlaid with gold, silver, and jewels. It had 127 columns, each representing a king. This temple is mentioned in Acts 19:35.

303

Tapestry of the Colossus of Rhodes

The Colossus of Rhodes

This was a 105-foot bronze statue of the sun god Helios, built in 280 B.C. on the island of Rhodes, in the Aegean Sea. It was built to commemorate a great victory. But 56 years later, it was toppled by an earthquake. The Apostle Paul stopped at Rhodes on his final journey to Jerusalem, but the statue would have lain in ruins on the ground then.

Alexandria, Egypt

The Pharos at Alexandria

This immense lighthouse was built on the island of Pharos near Alexandria, Egypt, in the third century B.C. It stood more than 400 feet high, had 300 rooms, and held a fire that burned day and night at the top. A huge mirror reflected the light. The Jews who translated the Hebrew Bible into Greek at Alexandria would have seen this great structure.

The Fertile Crescent

The Fertile Crescent is a large arc that encompasses the fertile river valley system of the Tigris and Euphrates rivers in Mesopotamia. It then curves northwest and south to include the eastern seaboard of the Mediterranean (Palestine), and, by some definitions, the Nile River Valley in Egypt.

Mediterranean coast

Rhodes

Nile River

The Island of Rhodes

Rhodes is a small island just off the southwest coast of Asia Minor, in the Aegean Sea. It was an important commercial center for traders, as it sat astride the shipping routes between the Aegean and the eastern Mediterranean. It did not have natural wealth of its own. Ezekiel mentions its trade with Tyre (27:15), and the Apostle Paul stopped there on one of his journeys.

Cyprus

Cyprus, off the coast of Lebanon, is the third largest island in the Mediterranean. It was rich in natural resources, especially silver, copper, and lumber. Jewish colonies developed there in the period between the testaments, and Paul encountered more than one synagogue there during his first missionary journey (Acts 13:5). The Gospel gained an early foothold there.

The Nile River

The Nile is the world's longest river, extending about 4,160 miles. Nestled in a narrow valley, it was the lifestream of the great Egyptian civilizations: 96 percent of the population lived within 12 miles of the Nile. The Nile flooded annually, providing irrigation for growing crops in the otherwise arid desert.

Cyprus

Jordan River

"The Baptism of Christ" by G. Cozzarelli

The Jordan River

The Jordan originates 1,200 feet above sea level north of the Sea of Galilee, near Mount Hermon, and descends to the Dead Sea some 1,300 feet below sea level. It is in a straight-line course of 120 miles. The river winds extensively for 135 miles in the 65-mile section from Galilee to the Dead Sea. The river descends quickly, has many rapids, and its current is strong.

The Red Sea

The Red Sea separates the Arabian Peninsula from Africa. At its northern end, its two branches define the Sinai Peninsula—the Gulf of Suez on the western side and the Gulf of Aqabah to the east. The term Red Sea comes from the Greek translation of a Hebrew term that probably means Sea of Reeds.

Happenings at the Jordan

The Bible records many events in or near the Jordan. Jesus was baptized there, and the Israelites crossed it on miraculously dry ground when they entered Canaan. In Joshua's day, an altar of stones was set up there to commemorate the crossing. The Jordan formed a natural boundary between Israelite tribes on both sides; another altar was erected to testify that God was witness to the friendship between the two sets of tribes.

Red Sea

The Sea of Galilee

This sea is located about 685 feet below sea level. It is a beautiful deep blue sea, with rugged hills rising abruptly from its eastern and western shores, about 2,650 feet above the lake's surface. Its position below sea level and flank of high mountains on the east make it susceptible to severe weather changes and great storms, some of which we read about in the New Testament.

Sea of Galilee

God's Delight

The beautiful harp-shaped Sea of Galilee is truly a wonder to behold. Its deep blue color, offset by the barren hills around it, gave rise to a rabbinic saying that "[the Lord] has created seven seas, but the Sea of Galilee is His delight."

"Moses Crossing the Red Sea" by Raphael

What Is the Sea of Reeds?

Many Bible versions indicate in marginal notes or in the Bible itself that the Red Sea was known as the Sea of Reeds. This is the most likely meaning of the Hebrew term. The most famous references to it are when the Israelites crossed it coming out of Egypt. These references probably refer to a northern extension of the Gulf of Suez or to a separate lake east of the Nile Delta.

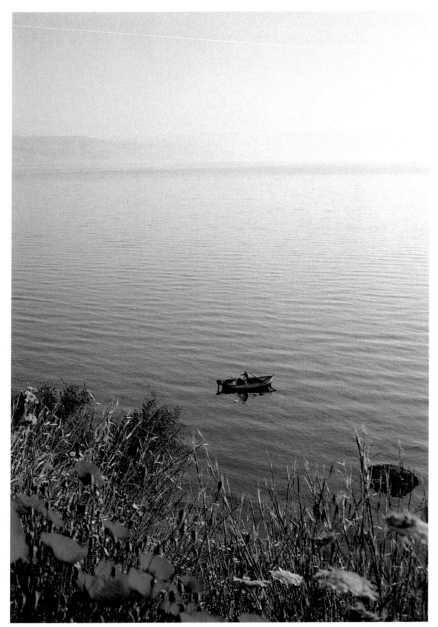

Sea of Galilee

Mount Sinai: The Mountain of Moses

Mount Sinai, where the Israelites camped and Moses received the Ten Commandments, is somewhere in the Sinai Desert. Its exact location is disputed, but the traditional site is a rugged peak in the southern part of the Sinai Peninsula called *Jebel Musa* (Arabic for "Mountain of Moses").

Mount Sinai

Joppa

The Sea of the Philistines: The Great Sea

The Mediterranean Sea had many names in the Old Testament. It was most often called the Great Sea, or simply the Sea. It also was called the Western Sea or the Sea of Joppa (Joppa was a port city). Once it is even called the Sea of the Philistines, since the Philistines lived on the coast in southwestern Canaan.

Relief of Roman merchant ship

The Mediterranean Sea

Palestine forms the eastern coastline for the Mediterranean Sea, a sea that stretches about 2,200 miles to the west. It allowed for great maritime civilizations to arise, such as the Egyptian, Phoenician, Greek, and Roman. It is mentioned many times in the Bible, but the Israelites were not a seafaring people and there were few natural ports on the Palestinian coastline, so it did not play a major role in Israelite history.

Phoenicia

Acts 21:2 mentions Paul setting sail from the Aegean for Phoenicia. This was the region covered essentially today by modern Lebanon—the coastal area north of Israel. Its principal cities in biblical times were Tyre and Sidon. The Phoenicians flourished in the first millennium B.C., especially as merchants and traders on the seas. They are usually referred to in the Old Testament as Tyrians, Sidonians, or Canaanites.

What Was Canaan?

In many Old Testament passages, the term Canaan refers to all the lands west of the Jordan (see Genesis 12:5), and, as such, it is fairly close to Palestine in its broader usage. In some Old Testament passages, however, Canaan refers to the Mediterranean coastland, especially Phoenicia, north of Israel (see Genesis 10:19).

What Was Palestine?

Palestine is the term popularly used today to describe the land that the twelve tribes of Israel occupied during biblical times. Its name comes from the name *Philistine*, and in the Old Testament the term designates only their territory, *Philistia*. By New Testament times, *Palestina* was a broader term, the title of a recognized Roman province. Since then, it has been a popular title for the Holy Land and has been used for 2,000 years. Even the British called this province Palestine in the early twentieth century.

Lebanon

Negev Desert

The Israelite "Destruction" of Canaan

In the popular mind, the Israelites invaded the land of Canaan and completely obliterated it with superior military force under Joshua. However, they only burned three cities: Jericho, Ai, and Hazor. Most of their conquests were accomplished by surprise attack or by God's miraculous intervention. Also, they left many Canaanites living in their territories, contrary to God's commands.

Mizpah: Biblical Retreat Center

At least six places were named Mizpah in the Old Testament, but the most important was south of Bethel, near Gibeon in Benjaminite territory. Its major significance was as a religious retreat center in the days of Samuel. Samuel called for a great day of fasting, confession of sin, and renewal at Mizpah after the Ark of the Covenant was recovered from the Philistines.

Ruins of Ai

Hazor: Capital Place

Hazor was the largest city built in Palestine in the biblical period. Its huge mound accommodated up to 40,000 inhabitants. It especially flourished in the second millennium B.C. as a great Canaanite capital. Joshua 11:10 indicates that "Hazor formerly was the head of all those kingdoms," indicating its place as political hub in Canaan at the time.

Ruins of Hazor

GEOGRAPHY

Beth-shean: Imposing Mound

Beth-shean (or Beth-shan) was a city in the Jezreel Valley, south of the Sea of Galilee. It has been occupied almost continuously from prehistoric times until the present. The accumulated debris of successive occupations has built up a large, impressive mound more than 70 feet high. It is most prominent in the Bible as the place where the Philistines hung Saul's dead body on their city walls (1 Samuel 31:10).

What Was Babel?

This was the Hebrew name for Babylon. It comes from the Babylonian *bab-ili* "gate of god." Interestingly, the story of the Tower of Babel relates the name to the Hebrew *balal* "to confuse," referring to when God confused the languages that people spoke. There is no linguistic connection between the two words, but the word play is an effective and arresting one.

The Great Ziggurat at Ur

A massive temple-tower (called a ziggurat) was built at Ur about when Abraham lived. It stood 70 feet high and had 3 levels. A temple to the moon god Nanna was at the top, and long staircases led to the first level. A temple to Ningal, Nanna's consort, was at the bottom. The remains of this ziggurat still stand, the best-preserved of the many that were built in antiquity.

Beth-shean amphitheatre

"Tower of Babel" by Jan Brueghel

311

Bethel: House of God

The name *Bethel* means "house of God." It was a town 12 miles north of Jerusalem, and it had an honorable reputation in Israel's early history. Abraham offered a sacrifice there, and Jacob had his famous dream there. During the period of the judges, it was an important worship center.

Bethlehem

Bethlehem and the Prophet Micah

The prophet Micah predicted Bethlehem's rise to prominence in a remarkable prophecy (Micah 5:2): "But you, O Bethlehem Ephrathah, who are little to be among the clans of Judah, from you shall come forth for me one who is to be ruler in Israel, whose origin is from of old, from ancient days."

Jacob's Dream

Bethlehem: House of Bread

Bethlehem means "house of bread." It is mentioned several times in the Old Testament, most prominently as the city where David was from, but its major importance was as Jesus' birthplace. Many holy sites have sprung up in Bethlehem, although the authenticity of many of them is questionable.

Bethlehem

Masada

Megiddo: Strategic City

Megiddo was a major Canaanite and then Israelite city in the Jezreel Plain in north-central Israel. It was located at the juncture of three major trade routes, commanding the main pass between the Plain of Sharon and the Jezreel Valley. As a result, it was the site of many important battles in Israelite history. An ivory plaque shows a prince of Megiddo receiving tribute and prisoners.

Masada

Masada is one of the most spectacular sites in the Holy Land. The city is on the flat top of an almost inaccessible rock bluff that thrusts dramatically upward from the wilderness floor near the Dead Sea. It was a fortified Jewish community that began in the second century B.C. The Romans had a garrison there about A.D. 6 until A.D. 66, when the Jews revolted and took it over again.

Masada

Jewish Zealots at Masada

Jewish Zealots forcibly occupied Masada in A.D. 66, and supplied it to withstand a long siege. It was the last Jewish stronghold to fall to the Romans during the Jewish revolt of A.D. 66 to 73. The Romans besieged it for seven months and built a ramp up the western side, where they breached the wall with battering rams. The 960 occupants inside all took their lives (except for seven women and children) in a suicide pact, rather than surrender.

Megiddo

Mosaic of Abraham and Isaac

Sparta: Jerusalem's Sister City?

Sparta was the capital of Laconia in southeastern Greece. Sparta is not mentioned in the Bible, but a Jewish tradition held that the Spartans and the Jews shared a common ancestry in Abraham (1 Maccabees 12:20). Friendly relations existed between the Spartans and Jews in the second century B.C.

Dalmatia: Home of the Firehouse Dog?

From 2 Timothy 4:10, we learn that Titus, one of Paul's companions, had left him to go to Dalmatia. This was a Roman district in what is today Croatia. It is thought to be the original home of the dalmatian breed of dog, the white-with-black-spots firehouse dog.

The Decapolis

This was a region of ten cities south and east of the Sea of Galilee. They were Hellenistic (Greek) cities loosely associated with each other, and were relatively free of Roman control. Jesus spent some time in the Decapolis, but much more in the region of Galilee.

Galilee

The Athenian Areopagus

This is a hill northwest of the better-known Acropolis in Athens. It was the site where murder cases were tried. The name also refers to the judicial council that met there at times. The Apostle Paul was taken there to be questioned about his teachings of Jesus and the resurrection (Acts 17).

Steps to the Areopagus in Athens

Philippi

Macedonia: Paul's First Stop in Europe

Macedonia was the first place in Europe that the Gospel was preached. It was a region of northern Greece and was for many years an independent kingdom. Its most glorious period came under Alexander the Great and his father Philip in the fourth century B.C. The Apostle Paul was moved to preach there by a vision in which a Macedonian man called him to come (Acts 16:9). Paul visited many cities there, including Philippi, Thessalonica, and Berea.

An Ancient Tel Aviv

The modern Israeli city of Tel Aviv gets its name from the ancient Telabib, an unidentified city along the River Chebar, the great irrigation channel near Babylon. Ezekiel visited the exiles at Telabib (Ezekiel 2:15). The Hebrew term means "hill of corn," but the same name in Babylonian means "mound of the flood."

Megiddo

Tel Aviv

Where Is Armageddon?

Revelation 16:16 states that Armageddon is a Hebrew word, but no such word is actually found in Hebrew. Many scholars think it stands for *har-megiddo* "mountain of Megiddo." Megiddo was the site of two decisive battles in the Old Testament between Israelites and foreign forces, and it might well have served as a symbol of the great final struggle between the forces of good and evil.

❧INDEX❧

Revised Standard Version, 58, 59, 136, 208
Rhodes, 304, 305
Rogers, J., 60
Roman Catholic Church, 37, 55, 88, 265
Roman Empire, 45, 47, 54, 88, 136, 147, 153, 215, 271, 277
Romans, 41, 154, 219, 224, 260, 263, 271, 281, 282, 313
Romans, Book of, 47, 51, 100, 105, 189
Rome, 268, 297
Rose of Sharon, 144
Rosetta, 87
Rosetta Stone, 87
Rosh Ha-Shanah, 160, 173
Round Table, 170
Russian, 216
Russian Public Library, 61
Ruth, 238
Ruth, Book of, 16, 205, 207, 238

S
Sabbath, 156, 159, 162, 163
Sadducees, 262
Salome, 264
Samaria, 63, 93, 120, 125, 208, 250
Samson, 15, 126, 134, 168, 181, 187, 213, 238, 240, 263
Samuel, 16, 110, 168, 217, 239, 240, 241, 310
Samuel, Books 1 and 2, 16, 17, 19, 23, 25, 39, 84, 131, 139, 140, 166, 171, 213, 217, 225, 240, 241, 243, 281, 288, 301, 310, 311
Sanballat, 250
Sanhedrin, 184, 261, 270
Sapphira, 270
Sarah, 37, 52, 233, 263, 301
Sardinia, 297
Sargon II, 93
Satan, 107, 110, 124, 258, 259
Saturn, 187
Saul, 16, 17, 23, 39, 70, 178, 217, 240, 241, 243, 266, 301, 311
Saul of Tarsus, 266
   (See also *Paul [apostle]*)
Scottish Church, 61
Screwtape Letters, The, 145

Sea of Galilee, 125, 214, 220, 300, 306, 307, 311, 314
Seaman's Version of the Bible, 60
Second Vatican Council, 88
Sela, 298
Seleucid Empire, 114
Sennacherib, 83, 93, 253, 296, 298
Septuagint, 18, 54
Sermon on the Mount, 104, 111, 188, 191
Seth, 69
Seven Deadly Sins, 188
Seven Wonders of the Ancient World, 182, 302
Shadrach, 32
Shalmaneser III, 86, 93, 139
Shamgar, 238
Shear-jashub, 255
Shechem, 176
Shelemiah, 250
Shem, 80
Shema, 150
Shiloh, 176
Sidon, 309
Sikkuth, 187
Silas, 299
Simon (brother of Jesus), 264
Simon the Magician, 272
Simon the Zealot, 263
Sinai Desert, 177, 210, 283, 284, 308
Sinai Peninsula, 306, 308
Sirach, Book of, 27
Sisera, 14
Sodom, 196, 280
Solomon, 18, 27, 38, 69, 117, 138, 139, 141, 147, 153, 154, 157, 204, 208, 217, 245, 246, 275
Solomon's Temple
   (See *Temple in Jerusalem*)
Song of Solomon, 28, 134, 144
Spain, 297
Sparta, 314
St. Ambrose, 74
St. Augustine, 74
St. Jerome, 54, 56, 122
St. Petersburg, 61
St. Peter's Fish, 125
Star of Bethlehem, 208
Star of David, 222
Statue of Zeus at Olympia, 302, 303

Stephen, 271
Stoics, 267
Sumerian Empire, 201, 283
Sumerians, 76, 87, 273
Sumerian King List, 232
Susanna, 39
Syria, 77, 149, 294, 272, 276, 314

T
Tabernacle, 8, 152, 153, 156, 175, 176, 236
Tabernacles, festival of, 159, 160, 170
Tabitha, 44, 272 (See also *Dorcas*)
Talmud, 63, 64, 65, 150, 153, 162
Tamar, 202
Tanakh, 58, 63
Targum of Job, 18
Tarshish, 297
Tarsus, 282
Tel Aviv, 315
Tell Deir Alla, 85
Tell el-Amarna, 89
Temple in Jerusalem, 25, 36, 39, 71, 75, 93, 103, 114, 141, 145, 147, 148, 149, 150, 151, 152, 153, 154, 155, 156, 157, 161, 175, 176, 209, 219, 233, 245, 256, 264, 275, 293
Temple Mount, 155, 156, 250, 287, 290, 293
Temple of Artemis, 182
Temple of Diana at Ephesus, 302, 303
Ten Commandments, 8, 12, 73, 85, 96, 152, 308
Thebes, 295
Thessalonians, Books 1 and 2, 49, 186
Thessalonica, 49, 315
Through the Looking Glass, 106
Thutmose, 236
Tiberias, 220
Tigris River, 90, 283, 296, 304
Tilapia, 125
Timothy, Books 1 and 2, 50, 106, 135, 268, 314
Titus, 50, 314
Tobiah, 154
Tobit, Book of, 37
Today's English Version, 58
Tomb of David, 289

Torah, 8, 12, 13, 66, 67, 75, 99, 148, 150
Tower of Babel, 296, 311
Treasury of the Pharoah, 299
Tree of Life, 140
Trinity, 13
Troas, 272
Turkey, 268, 274, 282
Tutankhamen, 236
Tyndale, William, 56, 57
Tyre, 305, 309

U
Ugarit, 181, 295
United States Marine Corps, 112
Ussher, James, 7
Ut-napishtim, 94
Uzziah, 299

V
Valley of the Cheesemakers, 287
Valley of the Kings, 295
Vulgate, 54, 56

W
Wailing Wall, 156
Wars of the Lord, Book of the, 28
Washington, George, 270
Western Wall, 156
Wicked Bible, 58
Wisdom of Sirach, 38
Wormwood, 135
Wycliffe, John, 56

Y
Yahweh, 8, 9, 14, 46, 157, 177
Yamm, 180
Yehohanan, 229
Yiddish, 84
Yom Kippur, 161, 173

Z
Zacchaeus, 70, 142
Zealots, 263, 313
Zechariah, 259
Zechariah, Book of, 31, 36, 121, 300
Zephaniah, Book of, 36
Zeus, 154, 180, 268, 302, 303
Ziggurat at Ur, 311
Zimri-Lim, 90
Zoroastrian religion, 277